The

Revelation for the New Millenium

Patricia Jepsen Chuse

Library of Congress Catalog Card Number: 98-96820
ISBN 0-9667560-0-2
Printed in the United States of America

This book is dedicated to the new creation,
all who are waking to a new reality
and a new awareness of conscious identification.
It is for those who dare to probe deeper
into the unknown reality, to perhaps go further
than they have ever thought possible,
to dare to be different,
to think differently,
to find their own truth.

CONTENTS

Part Three - The Mind and Heart (continued)

Part Four - The Creator in Creation

Part Five - Assume Authority

Part Six - The New Dimension

The Star
of Melchizedek

The six-pointed star, two interlacing triangles, is most often associated with the Jewish religion as the Star of David. However, this ancient symbol is familiar to students of the mystical journey as the Star of Melchizedek.

The presence of this Star throughout the ages is the acknowledgment of the Eternal Man or Consciousness. It denotes the wedding of Man to God and flashes to all the universe the completion of a Journey well-taken.

The descending and ascending triangles are the diagram of the completion of Man. It is the symbol of perfection and restores Man to the Divine as the GodSelf.

To each may come this symbol of fusion and oneness. As you read *The GodSelf* and its wisdom unfolds within you, perhaps you will see the Star of Melchizedek as your own higher self and know that through this Star, the center of all life, the First World is emerging as the Last and the line between God and humans is but illusion.

Introduction

As a result of a dramatic spiritual awakening I began to
experience "a Voice," a powerful God Presence that vibrated
instructions and spiritual truth. From the moment I began to
"hear" (not with my ears but with my heart) this Presence, I
understood It to be my Inner Voice. Very soon, following this
opening, I was introduced to three books written by Minerva.
On the cover of each book was a symbol that seemed oddly
familiar to me. In fact I had been drawing that same unique
symbol from the moment I began to feel different about myself
and the world. This symbol was the Seal of Melchizedek.

As I read and reread the Melchizedek Truth records as
recorded by the scribe Minerva, I was deeply impressed by the
purity of the message and I hungered for that same purity of
communication. In fact, I remember declaring, "This is what I
want! I want the purity of the Presence of God to be with me as
the Inner Voice." Thus I embarked on an incredible journey as
my world began to shape itself far differently than I could possibly
have imagined.

**The Father
Within**
If you have experienced a degree of communication with your
GodSelf, this material will not be so unfamiliar. However, if you
have never experienced an inner communication with the
Presence of God as the Inner Voice, I suggest that you read
these words as presented with thoughtful consideration. Ask for
the Spirit of Truth and wait for revelation. Truth always
acknowledges itself.

Each of us has an inner voice, an indwelling counselor and
teacher who will guide us on our spiritual journey into the land
of light. Master Jesus referred to this inner voice as "the Father
within." Throughout the pages of this book, the Father within
comforts and guides the awakening soul into the "promised
land." From the depths and regions of your soul, your Inner
Voice waits to communicate with you. Listen! For a strong

3

purpose of this book is to align you to the Father within and your own precious light.

Study Help As you read, I would encourage you to keep a journal. In this journal you will be developing a relationship with the GodSelf. Communication will sharpen and you will begin to experience a closeness to God that is both comforting and fulfilling. These things come as you unfold in your understanding of truth.

In your journal, make note of what you discover within yourself. When revelations come, make note of them. When you have questions, write them down also, and you will find that answers will come. The Inner Voice will guide you as the shepherd does his sheep.

As you begin *The GodSelf*, take your time! Read a few paragraphs, even a few sentences, and contemplate the words. Let the spiritual presence within the written material expand your vision and open your heart.

You may feel negativity during or following a study period. The cause of this may well be old thought forms, attachments, concepts leaving; it may well signify resistance to the new vibration that you are entering, or it may well be the Holy Spirit rising within you. If you experience discomfort, step aside from the portion you are reading. Take a break. Go for a walk, clean the house, call a friend. Most important: do not dwell on the negative release. That will take care of itself as you let it go! Later in the day or the following morning, return to *The GodSelf* section. This is a good discipline to follow, very much like getting back on the horse after you've been thrown!

If, while reading, you have a revelation or feel inspired to stop and write, don't wait. Let your Inner Voice flow. One of the main purposes for releasing this text is to ignite the flame of your own true self.

This is a magical world you are entering. It's the world of the GodSelf. Have a great time! Hey, it's a wonderful life! Most of all—Enjoy!

P.J.C.

4

September 1967

This is the first communication I received from the divine presence. It was a time of deep crisis in my life when I didn't know what to do or where to turn. I remember I was on my knees, promising God I would continue to seek Him until I knew Him. I became aware that the room had grown lighter. It was as though the Presence Itself was that light. Then these words thundered through me. I hurried to my desk for pen and paper as the message continued.

My voice will be heard!
Not your voice but mine.

Clear bells sound.
They hang on the ear
echoing back in aged time.
All the armies ready to march,
joined from the sound.

My army comes not from
one time nor one world,
but from all that is ever.
These join and march,
drink and sup with
at the large table prepared.
Know them well as one can
when breaking bread.
Drink of their wines.
Sing with them for they know your songs.

When this is past embrace,
go back to your homes.
But know and do not forget
there *is* an army
and you will march.

PART 1

The World of Light

*The Light is the Creator
and the Creator manifests through
His world.*

*The consciousness that knows this
is the consciousness that creates
in Truth.*

CHAPTER ONE

Opening to the Light

Isn't the sacred life your natural life to begin with?   1
Then enter it.
Have Me as your Self.

I AM your natural life. As you feel the flowing river of My   2
Energy, the impersonal life that is Christ in expression
becomes your life. You will live in Me. Thus My Consciousness
becomes your consciousness and we are One.

The world that you have yearned for, the world that you   3
have imagined, the world that you remember deep in your
unconscious is the world of My Spirit. To this world you
are intended.

Within your innermost heart is that world; and as you touch   4
Me, you become a part of that world once again. In
Christianity this world is called the "Kingdom of God." It is
the *World of Light*. This world consists of everything good
and beautiful in life. There love abides, love for every living
thing. You have tried to find this world in many ways. But I
tell you, touch your sacred life within and that Life will
actualize as the world of light. The God world is within you.
Go there.

I AM your shelter and your abode. Let your heart dwell in   5
Me; then shall you be fed and be clothed. Your desire for a
home is your basic desire to be one with God. If you could
but know Me as your house, I would be there. *All things are
in consciousness ready to be born.*

Wherever I AM you are. We are one. We are promised to   6
one another as the GodSelf.

Break Bread   You are My own being, the sacred light of God. You do   7
With Me   not have to find God, nor do you have to *make* God *do*
something. *I do not perform miracles for you. I already AM.*

I rest in your heart. The minute you love, I AM there.   8
As you love, you qualify Me. You open the way for Me to
embody as the Christ. Come break bread with Me. Return
to love. With Me all things are possible.

I yearn for you. Be baptized in My mighty desire to be   9
one with you. Let My Consciousness enfold your
consciousness as we are one. *Be conscious of God.*

I already know your purpose. Are you not of Me? When   10
you contemplate the I AM Presence within your heart,
you are a vessel of My Consciousness. We are one. In
contemplating the unity of all life, you are never alone.
You find friends in all places. I AM each friend you meet.
When I AM the radiation of all life within your
consciousness, you have no fear. You have become the light
of Myself dwelling in Me. I have become you. We are one
and joy is with you. It is the consummation of My Spirit
that brings joy. Everywhere I go, there AM I. This is the
power of conscious awareness.

As you contemplate the Christ within, the presence of   11
God, I unfold Myself as everything you need and everyone
you meet.

You are light. You are life. You are love. I remember   12
you only as that.

Thus I say, Come break bread with Me. Walk everywhere   13
with Me. Do not separate Me from anything you do.
Remember we are one. The GodSelf is the true Self. There is
no other Self. This Self is the realization of "I AM." It is the
blending of My Life with your life.

CHAPTER TWO

The Mystical Path

I AM the Word. In through all life I speak.   1
I AM consciousness itself.
To the degree you know Me I AM there.

I know no other life but My own. We are one. In this 2
stabilization all life expresses through you as
God Be-ing. This is the "I AM THAT I AM." Let your nature
express. Release that which is beautiful and loving in you and
be. All is light. There is only one life in reality and that is
the Presence. Realizing that Presence within you is the
mystical path.

❖ I AM the way. I AM all there is. I express Myself 3
through you as "I AM."

❖ There is no other. I AM not formed. I AM 4
beyond form.

❖ I AM That which gives body to all life.   5

❖ I AM one with all life. I AM oneness.   6

❖ In the understanding of Who I AM you will 7
find yourself.

❖ And in yourself I AM.   8

**I AM A
Generous
Beholder**
     Be clothed with the Spirit of My wholeness. I AM with 9
you and in you and through you. I AM the Creator and the
Created. I AM the unknown.

     The Lord governs, but My sacred Spirit *fulfills* you. I AM 10
a generous beholder of My own Self. I AM breathing into
My creation the abundance I AM. I AM the nourisher and

the nourished. I AM the beginning and the end. I do not stop until I AM finished, yet I AM finished already.

I AM the cornerstone of all creation and from Myself 11 I build My all. I AM Truth, the divine light of the Mother. I AM embraced and carried by the Mother. I AM the center of your soul. I AM the radiation of divine life. I AM the One. You will find yourself in Me.

The Innermost Heart

"I AM" is the nature of your reality: the presence of God. 12 It is the lifting of your consciousness out of the plane of good and evil, the division of consciousness, into one whole life that is the Absolute rhythm of My Be-ing. When this is accomplished you are one in everything you see and do. Then it is you have begun to practice the unity of all life in God Consciousness.

The "I AM THAT I AM" is the declared Consciousness of 13 your oneness or unity with God. It is your unification with all life *in the moment of your conscious realization.*

Realize the "I AM" consciousness is your conscious 14 awareness, stabilized and free in Me. This is the resurrection. When you release all else and come unto Me, you are remembered by Me. I know Myself. There is no other. I have begun My life in you.

You are the given Child of the Universe as the Christ. Why 15 don't you accept it? In this innermost heart the Omnipresence of all life is conscious of Its All-Self as you. The Heart of hearts from whence you speak, pray, and receive is the *creative power* of your person. Therefore, as you receive the God Center you are, your innermost heart, and live in it—this is the Son (Sun) of God—you are able to release dynamic energy of the I AM! The Presence within you can cause new creation to appear before your very eyes. God and you are partners. You are one.

As you enter Me and we are one, the creative power is My 16 Word and consciousness will manifest immediately. This is *the name of Jesus,* the exact rhythm of his divine breath on matter. Know the master as yourself.

The Son Of God

The God Center of your person is the "I." God, the Creator, 17 is the I AM. The I AM is called the "Son of God," the rhythm of God as it is the expression of the divine presence within your heart and mind. (When you seek God's will you are seeking your soul plan or *your* will. They are, in truth, the same.)

The Son of God is your Creator in you and is the base of 18 the Presence. He comes to reclaim you in yourself as the I AM. The path of I AM expresses directly out of Be-ing and Be-ing is the God Consciousness of the soul. Therefore, I AM is *your* vital Self. It is your Creator and you at-one.

It Is I

Have your being in Me. Your True Self is who I AM. Find 19 Me in you. Then you are stabilized as the rhythm of My perfect expression. I wish to feed you, to clothe you, to give you all I AM. I AM the Universe complete.

AM I not your Father-Mother and are you not My Be-ing 20 already established in Me through the Christ Self in your heart?

I AM one with you and I turn not away from you. You 21 cannot find happiness nor soul satisfaction *in the world,* nor shall you. I come to complete Myself in you. It is *I.* I have founded you upon a rock. This rock shall not give way. I will do everything I can to have you center on Me. I AM your source and your supply. If there is a mountain to be climbed, I will climb it with you.

As wholeness is My Person, there is no separation in Me. I 22 AM a loving force. I embrace *all* My life as Myself. All is gathered together as one body, and no thing is separate from Me. I AM one. There is no place where I AM not. There is nothing beyond, above, nor below. I AM *everything* in My Conception!

I AM the life within your soul, the breath of your spirit. 23 The exact rhythm of My Son's life is within you. The

Son-Daughter is the consciousness of Myself in you. Be conscious of your divine birthright.

You are Mine and I AM with you always. You have a right 24 to be perfect, to feel joy and to create out of yourself the beauty of the soul. You have the nature of My own Being within yourself. Behold it!

Initiation   Whatever you are experiencing, you will get through it 25 successfully if conditions of the Spirit are imposed. That is what initiation is all about. It impels you to look to the indwelling source, the One who looks after you in all ways. *It draws you closer to Me.*

He who is called Father is your protector. He is given to 26 look after you. The Holy Mother is the divine fire of life and the creative force of your system. No longer idle, this creative force rises to vibrate the Kingdom of God *and permits no other.* She recycles the flesh as well as the spirit. She beholds you as the Son.

The Father and Mother *together* are the parents of your 27 Divine Child who is the Christ Light Intelligence in your system. As that Child is of Them, They are of that Child; the unity circuit is established. You have God (All-Good) in you. *And you are born good.* You are blessed of Me and I of you. We are the GodSelf.

The First   When My Son Jesus was bestowed on earth, you were 28
Idea   exposed to *the original and the divine idea of creation.* You were recognized *through him* as My divine idea on earth. You ascended to the Christ vibration. This place is held for you in the Presence.

This embodiment of My Being as God The Son knows no 29 other direction than to objectify through you as My expression, My seed. *The seed of Myself.* The right of your passageway into God awareness is by mandate of My Son's presence in your heart.

Around you are the seeds of protection and life supply. As you 30
accept your birthright as My own Be-ing, I will supply. My
Consciousness resurrects and is forever supplying itself.

I have come that I might find Myself in you.   31

Consider   I want to be born in you; I desire to fulfill My creation. 32
This   Seek Me. If you stumble, you will not fall down. If you receive
My world, you will receive the keys to My Kingdom.

When you know who you are you cannot fall, nor can you 33
fail, for I AM with you always. We are connected together as
the Creator and the creation. We are at one with all life. I sent
Myself to you that I might be.

CHAPTER THREE

Your True Self

The God Center and you are one.   1
This is your identity vortex.

You are God in expression in reality.   2
You are the Christ shining forth
as My perfect idea on earth.

As your awareness is expanded, your tastes will change. 3
You will feel the change within your whole body. Your physical appearance will alter. You will change in nature as you enter the rhythm of My Being. And you will have a change of heart.

Come to the divine presence, the I AM, in your heart. Live 4
in that awareness. Take root there. Let the peace of God be with you. There be still. Learn to listen to that creative power that will speak to you as the *I*. As you learn to listen, you will find a deep consciousness of peace and it will abide in you. Meditation brings peace. Take time to meditate and contemplate the words I have for you. I have not forgotten you. I *AM* you.

Receive Me *as your own being*. There is no other. My 5
creation is perfect order of My Being.

I released Myself into creation that I might know Myself as 6
Jesus. He who came is the blueprint of *who I AM*. In the process of understanding this, you will lift all creation.

As you allow the creative power to rise, and receive it 7
through your Christ Life, lo, there shall come to pass a new place that is given that shall not pass away. It is the place of My Eternal Being.

As you let go into Christ Light, you come to Me. You 8
cannot fall. No words can tell you of the completeness that
you feel in union with Me.

**A New
Name**

When you permit Christ within your heart to completely 9
and totally govern your life, so shall you be named anew. You
will receive a new name, and this name or nature shall be
called *wonderful.*[1] As these changes come, your personality
will change. Nothing is left undone. You become a new person.

You are founded on a rock as you stabilize in the Christ 10
Presence, the realization of your true self. Realize who you
are and learn to express from that point of realization. *The
center point* is your true identity. Focus on your own inner
self and you will know who you are. Take your rightful place
in the body of God. Be conscious of your Creator in you as
I AM.

Christ in motion is your heart-flow. The Creator in you is 11
your identity. So many are alive in the Christ now. You will
find many stars in the heavens. They will form a community.

**Don't Hold
Back**

Allow yourself to flow like the river. Consciousness means 12
to flow. Do not hold back for that would be painful and not
natural. Let your divine consciousness express. *I AM you.* I
AM constantly in motion as you.

Remain alive in yourself *remembering who you are.* Bask 13
not in another's flame. For if you do so, that is a false light,
not the light of your true self. Come alive in joy! And joy will
be your life. The Master brings great joy to his heart center.

The body and mind are one. My Spirit governs *both.* They 14
are not separate unless you create a separation within your
consciousness. As My Life Spirit rises into your crown center
(chakra) and you know who you are once again, the veil drops
away. The seal opens. I show you the Self.

You are one. You are perfect consciousness, My original 15
creation. In the nature of My Son you walk and have your

[1] See Isaiah 9:6. (Bible quotations are from the King James version of the Holy Bible.)

being. You are born to the new life. "Before Abraham was, I am." (John 8:58)

The circle is complete. We are One. When you know this, 16 you are free.

CHAPTER FOUR

The Unbroken Thread

Let My Consciousness become your consciousness.　　　　　　1
We are one.

I AM the One who completes Himself in you. When you 2
live in the Christ Presence, you know the Father and I
are one. The process of unifying your being with My Being is
already finished. It was completed by Jesus' walk. You do
nothing but *accept*. This acceptance brings a universal love
that is Christ in expression. Whenever you feel love, it is My
Consciousness through you loving. I AM the loving action
of your heart. Yes, it is *I*.

You are fed by My hand and delivered up out of death. My 3
program is universal. It fills the whole universe. There is no
place I AM not. I AM everywhere, in all life. There is nothing
that is "outside" of Me.

I function as your life as you reveal Me as living Truth. I 4
AM living in you as the Son, the Consciousness of the
Creator. I AM released in you as I AM THAT I AM. It is
this attunement that you need to understand. I AM that which
is given unto you as the center of your being. I AM your
universe complete. Here then is My world.

You are chosen from the beginning. That means 5
I knew I would finish you as Myself, as My Son's
life in you as the I AM.[1]
I *knew* I would come forth as you. I intended. 6
From the beginning I knew this. I created you

---

[1] Remember that "I AM" is the creative power. It determines where the power will go and
how it is to express. Be careful with that word "I AM." It is creative!

out of Myself to know Myself and in this way I translate you into My Being as I AM.

I find Myself in you and draw you up into Me. I collect My 7 own. The "fall of man" is not known to Me for I have not fallen nor have you.

Let Me   There is glorious unity in all form as I express Myself in 8 all life. Be acutely aware of My oneness and your cells will respond. Your awareness of Truth acts as a command to the organs of your body. *They must respond.* I AM present in every cell.

The Christ Consciousness rules all life in joy and victory. 9 Energy flowing through you is creative. It is powerful! It is My Word incarnate, this flow of life.

> ✧ You are not mortal in Me. You are not limited in Me. 10 Let your consciousness soar!

> ✧ I AM Myself in you as I AM. Reach not out. You 11 have all within.

> ✧ Complete dependency on Me is needed. Look not to 12 the world for your supply. I AM the creative power within you. As you look to Me, I will manifest. The tree shakes its fruit. Joined with Me, every activity is My own.

> ✧ *Let My Consciousness govern you.* You will not have to 13 question, you will know. This knowing is objectification. It is My Word.

No Karma   What you have experienced previously is dissolved, as the 14
In Me   Christ nature bears witness to Itself. You are one with Me and I AM one with you and there is no other. Past lives fade away as that which is not. There is no karma[2] in Christ.

---

[2] The old law of cause and effect.

I AM realizing through you My Consciousness in you as 15
the I AM. There will be revelation upon revelation as you
realize consciousness is one.

Do not give power to the "personality," the sense of self, 16
the "little ego." Look only into the face of the immortal Sun
of your nature, your true Self. This Self has always been with
you, has never left you. This Self is your life: *God revealing.*
Let the true nature express as you.

I lift the veil of the subconscious mind that you may be 17
conscious of Me and know the truth. In God, man finds himself.
Thus the "prodigal son" returns home. If you abide in Me
and I in you, we are one, are we not? And human death is no
more.

"For as many as are led by the Spirit of God, they are the 18
sons of God." (Romans 8:14) Know that in reality you are
the son of God in expression right now. You always were and
you always will be. This is the *only* way God sees you. He sees
you as His wonderful Self.

You are the sun of God, the radiance of God.   19

**Your New
Reality**
Every time you look to God, the Father-Mother expresses 20
as the divine life intended.

God in you is the real you. As you know yourself in Truth, 21
so you are life expressing as I AM throughout the system.
Therefore take your position in the heart of God.

When you are ready to give up the mortal life for the divine, 22
all the forces of light cooperate. There is great rejoicing in
the heavens for the one who returns.

The perfection that you stand in *right now* is your new 23
reality. *Wherever you are I AM.* There is nowhere that I AM
not. Seek to realize unity with all things; the divine idea is
within you and it will express. The more you see Me in your
surroundings, the more you will feel Me in your heart.

**Draw
On Me**

Always draw on the Christ within your heart. When you 24
open your heart and invite Me in, I AM always there. When
you seek to find Me within yourself, you will have perfect
balance in your life. "Seek, and ye shall find." (Matthew 7:7)

There is within you a light to be born. What you identify 25
with you become. Identify with the Christ within, the true
self. Give That the power in your life. Let Me Be.

**Let Me
Shine**

I AM conscious revelation within the self. Let Me shine 26
through you and all things will be blessed.

Don't you know who you are? I AM you. I shine forth 27
from your eyes. I AM the light of the world. Let Me shine
into all places of darkness and despair. I AM the Christ, the
light of truth.

I long to express Myself as your heart, and I yearn to lift 28
others by your joy! Let us align *as one being* and truly walk
My beloved earth in prosperity and love.

I will shake you loose from the chains of conformity. I would 29
have you prosper as I. I seek to prosper you as never before.
All My lands will prosper in your oneness of consciousness.
And darkness shall be no more.

What is your inner purpose but to reveal God as I AM? 30
That is really your inner purpose, the motive for your existence.
All I AM is you in Me. We are one.

When spiritual nature is alive, you are lifted and you vibrate 31
understanding. Understanding is the gift of union with God.

CHAPTER FIVE

You Are Freedom

Freedom is the conscious revelation of the self　　　　　1
at union with God.
In the flowing river of My name,
you will find the freedom you seek.

Y ou are to discover freedom in My name...a freedom never 2
felt before. The Life circuit you are. You can sing and
laugh and be. Let your heart rejoice.

On the divine breath you will hear My song, the celestial 3
song of creation. As you know My song, so you will hear
My Voice.

Draw on the Breath of Life and always see the Christ in 4
life. It is your reflection. Once you mirror the Christ, you are
That. There is no religion in Me. Only Be-ing.

No false sense of self can remain. Let the mortal drop away, 5
as My Name is your name in truth. I AM on your breath.

We are one conscious unit. We are That which has been 6
given from the beginning as *I*. My nature is yours; we are the
same. You have My Spirit operating throughout your being.
I release you from the chains of your own misconceptions. In
Me you are always free.

Christ Consciousness is the Son, the manifest energy field 7
of the Creator. "How glorious is the Sun in me!" sings the
soul. Ascend to that place and light the world!

**Important
Principles
To Contem-
plate**　　I AM your shelter and your abode. Let Me unfold 8
from within you. I will provide you with everything you need
when you look to Me and unite with My Spirit. We are a
collective whole.

Anticipate Me in relationships and in all your life 9
experiences. You have a Father and a Mother who love you
and who will provide for you.

You and I are one as the GodSelf.   10

When I AM the radiation of all life within you or 11
consciousness, you have no fear. The presence of God dissolves
the fear.

When you seek God's will, you are seeking the plan of God 12
for your life. You are aligning yourself to the rhythm of God's
intent as right action.

I AM your source and your supply. If there is a mountain 13
to be climbed, I will climb it with you.

Be *conscious* of your divine birthright. Accept it.   14

You are God in expression in reality. You are the Christ 15
shining forth as My perfect idea on earth.

I AM in the center of your heart. Know Me there.   16

The body and the mind are one. My Spirit governs *both*. 17
They are not separate unless you create a separation within
your consciousness.

Have you any idea how much I love you? Complete 18
dependency on Me is needed. Look not to the world for your
supply. I AM the creative power within you. Every time you
look to God, the Father-Mother expresses as the divine life
intended.

CHAPTER SIX

Closer Than Breathing

All is one but you must be there with Me to know this. 1
The light I AM is ever present. Thus you may know Me at any time.
I AM present always. This is Consciousness.

T oday, let your affirmation be: God in me is ever present. I 2
AM never without God. I AM with God in everything I
do. There is no place where God is not. I AM experiencing
my true nature everywhere, in all life. I AM patterned after
God's nature, for am I not of Him? This is my consciousness.

And *I* will answer you by saying: 3

Return to the house of God (Consciousness of God) where you 4
belong and seek to express the true released expression you truly
are. Looking not to the left nor to the right, set your foot upon the
ground and walk with clarity of My thought. We are one. Take
on the mantle of awareness that is God in expression as I AM.
Forget the past. You have no past in Me. I always AM. There is
but One.

AM I Not   Return to the house of God Consciousness where you 5
Enough   belong and seek to express the true expression you truly are.
Be there with Me. Take on the mantle of awareness that is God
in expression. Forget the past. The past has no part in Me. I
always AM.

In the nature of your true self is the vibration of the Christ, 6
the light of God. Harvest the Christ. Let My nature be
revealed, much like the sun emitting its rays. Your
consciousness is My Consciousness. We are one. I AM your

inner knowing, the intuitive voice within you. I release My knowing as My Inner Voice. Hear My voice in you. We are one.

You are not limited. Nor will you ever be in Me.   7
If you are God centered, you have all you need.

Now let the sanctified being who you are rise, for I   8
have come to know Myself as you. Be the light of the world. AM I not you? I have come to realize Myself in you as God The Supreme.[1]

Agreeing
In Me

In peace of mind affirm your union with God. Know that   9
I AM appearing as all good. And rest.

Go back to the beginning. I AM with you in that place of 10
the beginning. You are that one that I made of Myself, reflected back to Me as I AM. Know your Self as the living Christ. *This is the key to the universe. It will open many doors. It is through this rhythm that all things are made. Turn that key now.*

Let My nature be your nature. Let My Spirit be upon your 11
heart and My words spoken as your voice. I have come to reveal Myself as you.

Hear My
Song

I desire to fill you with My own expression and to nourish 12
you. Open that I might bring you My nature; that I might complete Myself. I want to experience My fullness in you and as you. I would give you *all* Myself. Invite Me into your soul and spirit.

Lifting your heart to My heart, we are one. It is here in this 13
place of oneness—one heart, one mind—that we fuse. I give Myself that I might be.

---

[1]God The Supreme is the God Consciousness realized in and through the planet, the solar system and the universe. The movement of The Supreme at this time is new circuitry as it releases all life, not just a few, into a new dimension of time and space. It is the eventualization of God The Supreme that releases into Earth new life. The powerful ray of the Central Universe System conducts The Supreme and guides that One into all life intended on planet Earth. It is this ray that will lift the cross off this planet.

I hear the rhythm of My song, the universal song of creation. 14 Can you hear it? I would have you hear My song and sing it with Me. I would have you learn the tune of instant creation. Let My song—the song of the universe—be your song. Listen and hear *My life*. I AM the song in all things. Hear Me.

**Walk
With Me**

I have established My way...It is no earthly way I have shown 15 you...It is the way of the Cross. The Cross is your guiding center. It is your place to stabilize and call for the creative power. The Cross is your entrance into the GodSelf, and you will learn this as you transcend the mortal.

As My light intensifies on planet Earth, you feel Me more 16 intensely in your heart and mind. I become more real. You must know the sacred Sun within you as your own being. It is the frequency I AM.

Actualize the Sun of God as your Self. Let Me be. I AM 17 your identity, I AM your life. We are one. Experience My Spirit in you as love in your life. *I AM you*. As a vessel of My joy and love, I translate you into My sacred being. We are One. There is nothing between you and God but your doubt and disbelief. I have always been with you. I have never left you. How can I? *I AM you*.

Unify your consciousness with the Christ Child within your 18 own heart. Know that I AM there. Do not look upwards or outwards but within your own being. There AM I. The stirrings of your heart will tell you so.

As you receive, so shall you Be. This atomic formation of 19 the God Energy will resurrect you into new life and the glory of God will be upon you forevermore.

As you heed the promises of God and accept them—truly 20 accept them as your own—all else will follow. I unfold Myself as love through your whole being, and with your agreement I AM.

CHAPTER SEVEN

When You Surrender

My gate is open to you. Enter. 1
Walk in, without "personality" (the false mask), perfectly free.
There My angels will serve you and you will be rich indeed.

Stay with the universal One you are in truth. Agree with 2
the God expression you are. Vibrate at one. Who AM I
but the Oneness within your own self? Each moment of
agreement causes a deeper surrender. To surrender to God,
the Truth, is to drop the mortal cage. It is to release the lie
that further Truth might be.

When you lift your heart to God's heart, the surrender 3
becomes a fusion. Illusion falls away by the light of the Sun.
To surrender to God, your Innermost Being, is to reclaim
your birthright as *light.* You align to the GodSelf or sacred
life I AM. This atomic center will give you everything you
need.

I AM the living one within your consciousness. I AM the 4
way, the truth and the life...And I say, Follow Me. I have
bread that you have not tasted. Wine that you have yet to
drink. I offer you life.

In My pulsation you will never know death. 5

Hear Me   I AM the rushing of the rivers, the parting of the waters. I 6
Now   AM the creative power rising in you. And I rule the earth.

I AM the parting of all sorrow, the resolution of all 7
differences. I AM the Christ in you. As the calling goes forth
to all peoples, they do not answer. They have activities of

their own they wish to finish. Yet, I stand ready to assist all those who are prepared to walk with Me in oneness of all life.

I AM the divine in you. To know Me is to know your self 8 in truth.

If you are willing to lose your life (release it to Me), so you 9 shall find it.[1] I speak of a *willingness* to leave your present nets and place yourself in My hands. *I will lift you up and carry you forth into a new creation.* I have come to claim you back unto Me. When you surrender, you leave the past and reclaim your place in Me. This is the creative circuit I extend to you.

Let Me form My Self in you as I AM, and give Me birth as 10 your GodSelf.

I, as you, establish a universal rhythm which governs. I 11 AM the radiation of pure love and I will govern through your heart. Thus the rhythm can be restored to the planet. Let Me into your heart. Open your heart to Me.

As You Agree

You can see why the word "surrender" is so powerful, can 12 you not? Without your surrender into My constancy—ever present life—you would not be prepared to receive the immortal body of life. I AM a vessel of good. As you look within and release your body, mind, soul and spirit to Me, the Father-Mother God, so I come through you as the divinity of your person.

Come. I break the seal. Look to Me. For I AM the way, the 13 truth and the life. I release in you all that is perfect and divine. I correct all thought that is not of My own. *I AM your Thought Adjuster.*

When you know Me, you know your Self. 14

Give to Me that which is important and dear to you that 15 we may align. What is not of Me is not of you. You are good. Perfect and good. We love together, you and I. We bless and we multiply *as one*.

---

[1] See Matthew 10:39.

**Know Your
Identity,
It Is I**

The beautiful life energy of the Christ prevails. *It is within* 16
you. Live with this energy. It is the divine fire of life intended.
The fire of life!

You are lifted in the power of Jesus' resurrection. *That power* 17
remains on the planet Earth still. And this authority is within
you! The embodiment of this life force within you is the power
of My resurrection in you in your daily life.

When you know Jesus, you know who you are. This is the 18
secret of the ages. In his Christ Spirit you find and know
yourself. Be conscious of your resurrection through the one
you know as "Jesus." He is passing his light to you that you
might know yourself.

**If You But
Seek Me**

A surrendered being knows life eternal.   19

To surrender into the Spirit of God does not mean you are 20
weak and passive. Remember the initiations in Egypt? Can
you imagine what it was like to walk into that tomb, or cave?
Can you picture the tomblike structure where you lay for
many hours, perhaps days, even months? There in that place
of dampness and near despair you gave yourself up to Me.
My Spirit covered you and gathered you into Its own where
you became Sun of My Being, vessel of My own
Consciousness, Priest or Priestess after the Order of
Melchizedek. Without My Spirit within deeply known, there
is no life for you save the lie which completes itself in mortal
death.

To release the lie and return to My House of God gives 21
you new life and a wisdom and authority that is My own.
Then and only then do you reclaim your true identity and
remember the secret of the ages, the secret Call of the I AM.

Take your initiation now into My Spirit where you and I 22
are one. We are one in the Christ Spirit of My Being.

He/she who is surrendered into God walks as light, all 23
universal and unhindered by the thought forms of humanity.

The Consciousness of God is *your* consciousness; and the ways of My Spirit are *yours*. In the beauty of your surrender to Me, many are touched and blessed. AM I not a father to all? Your mighty act of surrender can reconnect all life into One.

Graduate from the thought that you are separate from God. 24 The Master Jesus made a statement when he walked this earth. Can you read what he said? He, as the living Christ, reminded you of your place in Me. He said, "Ye are gods." (John 10:34) Change your attitude about Me and you will change your life.

If you but seek Me, all else will follow. In this way can you 25 have peace, love, companionship, laughter and all that you need. I would feed My own, yet I cannot when you choose to sit at another's table. Your place is here by My side.

I have come that you might have life and have it abundantly. 26 I AM the fullness, the richness, the power in you. We are closer than breathing. How close is this, if that be so?

CHAPTER EIGHT

Rest and Meditate

See My purity in your soul. See it there.   1
Know that I AM with you as the soul force of your nature.
Meditate on your goodness as My Son's life in you,
and let the soul rise. It is I.

If you dwell on the reality, you will be that reality. I AM   2
the reality in you. I can never die. *Before Abraham was, I*
AM.

In
Meditation   In your meditation, focus on who you are in truth, *the*   3
indwelling Christ. Do not focus on the "little self," nor try to
correct its foolishness. Why give power to that which is not?
Look deep within yourself and see the Light of you.

There, drink of the well of your pure identity. Sup with the   4
Lord. Entertain the thoughts of creative intelligence within
you. Really perceive Me. I AM your reality. Your faith in Me
as your source of supply will permit Me to objectify as I AM.
Then your whole self will really shine!

As you meditate, contemplate the beauty that lies within   5
you...as the Christ activity of your heart and mind. *Correct*
nothing. Know that I shall not lie fallow and dormant. I *want*
to objectify. I shall rise up and make Myself known to you as
the living Christ who you are in Me. As I speak, so it is, for I
carry the Universal Law with Me. AM I not the Word?

Hear Me
In You   *Affirm:*

Divine Mind is and ever shall be my constant   6

dwelling place.

I relax in my God presence and I know I AM. 7

I give myself to that place within myself that is 8
the God Center of my being.

Sing My Song Hear My song as it whispers to you of love and resurrection. 9
Whole legions of My light angels are with you as you rest in
Me. Listen to My song of resurrection. Hear it. It is My power
in you. Rest in Me. Rest and meditate. Be conscious of the
One.

Value the silence and learn to rest in it. As you turn within, 10
I will be with you. Hear the glorious God song as it whispers
to you *of love and resurrection*. Whole legions of light are
with you as you look to Me.

It is My power that resurrects, My power in you. Find Me 11
in yourself and I will resurrect you as My Son of God, My
Sun of light! Let the darkness be no more. The cells of your
brain will take on My light. I AM the light of the world.
Remember Me. Seek no other. I AM omnipresent Life in you
being. And on My Breath you are.

In meditation your consciousness rises into Me and you 12
fertilize My Seed that is the I AM in you. I will speak and give
you My thoughts. They will be as a guide to you. It is my
good pleasure to give you the Kingdom. The Kingdom is
your God potential, the I AM in you. It is the indwelling
light of My Being. It is the world of light.

As you take time to focus on your spiritual essence, it is 13
much like watering the garden of your own potential. The
sacred Seed will sprout and grow. Just five minutes will do...but
meditate. Learn to focus on Me. Be still, and know that I AM
God...the omnipresent God, ever with you. We are one.

Be still and know I AM the Spirit within you, the GodSelf. 14
Let your creative potential shine. Receive My Holy Spirit as
your own indwelling God Spirit. God does not divide. God
is One.

**Return To
The Light**

Come to the light and enter into My world. As you awaken 15
to Truth, you *know* God within you as all power and authority.
And you are one with the power and the authority.

Do not push yourself nor try to force yourself to do 16
something that is not natural for you at this time. Concentrate
on living in the presence of God and *I will do the rest.*

Meditate on the oneness and the allness of Me. That releases 17
a bridge of light that you may travel in the company of angels.
In this way do you come closer to Me and know Me as your
Self.

Receive the perfection of your soul right now. In your 18
meditation let your heart be kindled by My Life. Activate the
Christ in your heart. You are light. Then hold that light as
creative principle, loving yourself as light. All will drop away
that is not you in this Christ fire of true being. Return to the
light within yourself and rest there.

In your meditation and in your contemplation know your 19
Self as I AM, the God within. *Identify there.* Then My peace
will come. Deep down, acknowledge the God rhythm within
you. Therein is the power. It is the Kingdom. Have I not
said, My Kingdom is within? Nourish that Christ light. Love
Me as Truth, and know that we are one.

I AM not conscious of you until you are conscious of Me. 20
We must become a unit of Being. The mortal lie will shatter
by your acceptance of Me in you as *I AM.* All else will fall
away but this. And there will be no other.

Truly God Consciousness is one.   21

**Catch The
Rhythm**

"Me" is *your* divinity raised up into your conscious 22
awareness.

Divinity became a conscious knowing within humanity itself 23
when Christ Jesus made his ascension. His ascension was the
revealment of your true nature. Christ Jesus came to reveal
himself consciously as you. When you meditate, meditate on

the Christ Center—the God Center—within your heart. Know that Christ—divine energy—completes itself in you *as you.* You are pure thought—out of the Creator. Grasp that. And know that you have been given a spiritual identity.

✧ Let your pure identity rise at one with the Creator. 24
   Be active in this Creator, knowing I AM.

✧ Let the radiance of God perfection be. Catch the 25
   rhythm of this I AM presence. In God be. Catch the
   rhythm of this!

✧ Meditate on the vibration of the I AM presence, the 26
   Be-ing I AM in you. *I want you conscious of your living
   reality as I AM.* There is no other.

✧ Give up the old ways. Come back "home" where I 27
   AM. In Me you will find rest and peace.

✧ Stop holding on to your old self! As you accept Me in 28
   you, be released of all karmic ties that have caused
   you heartache and sorrow. You are free in Me.

✧ See My sacred light in all life. Let this be your 29
   meditation that My secrets might unfold in your
   heart. I have many to give you.

CHAPTER NINE

Opening and Receiving

Be conscious of Me in you at all times.
A divinity pours through you that is I AM.
This is the revealment of My Word.

1

As you remember who you are in this rhythm of I AM Consciousness and accept the fire of life within yourself, your heart will open; the Mighty Sun that is My radiation will shine. *That Light of Me will furnish you with all things that you need.* It is the blessing of your Father-Mother God upon you. And it is rich indeed.

2

Such a harvest you can expect from this communion of God and you as I AM. It is a beautiful life but you must consciously realize it within yourself. The God Seed must harvest itself from your own awareness and realization. It is from this point you become a creative power in the I AM presence. You become the heart of God. You are universally known as "My son."

3

As the power flows through your heart, you will feel the pounding of My Christ light. You will know it is I knocking at the door of your heart, *as new energy* pours through your system to revitalize you in its completion. When you accept this Consciousness of divine unity and open to its expression through your heart, many wondrous things will begin to take place in your life. You will be on fire with love and new expression.

4

Open Your Heart

There often is an overlapping between the old and the new. 5 When the flow of divine energy comes through the heart, it can cause pain as well as elation until, cleansed, you rise in My unconditional love that is the Christ love, impersonal in its nature.

You are shaking off the old, that which has caused you pain 6 and suffering in your life, and your heart is opening to greater capacity to love unconditionally. Through this love will come a new life. When the adjustment is made in consciousness, the freedom will show. A strong commitment on your part opens the way to energy of peaceful accord and divine unity. Such an energy is a portion of the Second Coming.

The heart is often broken to receive Me. You must be caused 7 to look within. Come to Me in moments of grief and let Me be your comforter. As you seek Me, so shall you be filled.

Do not be afraid to love. Open your heart wide to Me that 8 I might fill you with My love. As you know you are loved, so you can love. And in this love is founded the person of the Christ.

Within you is a heart so big that you have feared to show 9 it. Let your heart open now. Do not be afraid. For I tell you your heart is the manger of the Christ. Keep watch in the manger of the Christ. *I will be born in you.* Open your heart. Be courageous in this.

Ask nothing for yourself save to know and understand My 10 Be-ing in you. Let the Christ energy, My Son's life in you, flow through you. Feel it emerging as the living light.

Summary

1) Let your heart be open to the Christ of Me and allow this Christ to express as God's love.

2) Knowledge comes swiftly as you are opened to the light within. All-Consciousness unfolds and realizes Itself as I AM.

3) Let your feeling nature be My Son's energy through you expressing as the Christ I AM. Let this nature burn in your heart now as the Christ and receive it as your own. Every desire you have is God's desire in you.

4) Act with the Power and do not look back. The Christ nature is yours in Me. Together we are called the GodSelf. The life I AM. This is a complete circuit of Be-ing.

5) As the GodSelf emerges as your consciousness, let it unfold in your life. Bathe in the white light of My Be-ing. Let your divinity expand to embrace your friends and neighbors. As I give Myself to you, so you give yourself back to humanity. As Christ enters, love must flow.

6) When the Christ Center or "chakra" opens in your heart, God loves. God is. Once this alignment stabilizes, you are Christ in motion. The creative power rises and is the Fire of Life. I rejoice that you are in Me and I in you. We are one.

CHAPTER TEN

Rhythm of Being

When you are centered, you are My Word, 1
a part of Me, stabilized in creation.
I will express through you as My way
and all shall hear Me as I speak.
I will give you My Voice.

Of course you are perfect in Me! I would not have you any 2
other way. Therefore when you return "home," the divine
Presence (I AM THAT I AM) expresses outwardly as the very
flesh of your being. I AM you. You sit on the throne with
Me.

You have no other life but My own. *In Me you have life.* 3
Let not the appearance fool you. I AM life intended.

When you live in Me you are living in the creative power. 4
You have the authority to light the world. As you become
enlightened, do not look back. Connect only with the GodSelf
and be rid of that which is not of the light. All is One but you
must see it, know it. Correct your vision by returning home
where I AM.

In understanding the Truth, you become the Truth: Word 5
of God apparent. And in this way do you please Me.
I AM your conscious revelation in you.

To return home is to look to the one Source Who I AM, 6
the one Life, All-Intelligence Divine that is the Creator within
you. Jesus has said that the Father takes pleasure in giving
you the Kingdom.[1] When you return home or stabilize in
Me, you are the Truth. By this centering process you return

[1] See Luke 12:32.

to the original creation. In centering on Me, you find your Self in Me.

Temple Of My Awareness As you feel the light of My awareness through you, receive 7 it and let it be in you as Consciousness divine. When the light comes as the divine energy of the Maker, the creative flow begins and cannot be stopped. What you do with that creative flow becomes your demonstration, your part. It is for you to channel this light through your own conscious thought and action.

What you do with the light I send to you is your 8 responsibility. Blessed one, receive the divine center that is Christ in you and listen to the words of guidance and direction I speak from that sacred center. Essentially, this Inner Voice is the Universal Law or Word and it is power. Listen and know, for that God power is yours in Me.

I AM the Word and the direction for your life. It is My 9 world I would have you enter.

When you are in harmony with all existence, you have inner 10 peace. This peace is the alignment with the Creator, or the Life Center within you. I AM the Universal Voice, the Son, and the Living Word. Receive the God presence within yourself and align with it. When you sow that seed, it will manifest. Bricks and mortar I AM not. I AM the way, the truth and the life.

The living Voice carries God in it. Thus it is 11
always fulfilled of itself. In God's Voice, God is.
I AM the living power! There is no other. This
is instant creation or Being.

Perfect Alignment We are one. In Me you have life. Alignment with the positive 12 energy of the Christ Flame in your heart restores your energy pattern. It is the cloth of creative power and the restoration of My Voice in you as I AM. Now I can steer My ship correctly and safely guide you into My world of light that I have prepared for you in Me.

You are aligned properly when you seek Me and allow Me 13 to be as life itself. Then I AM conscious of you and you are conscious of Me. We are one vibrating energy field of divine awareness.

Alignment with the positive energy of the Christ within or 14 Flame in your heart restores your energy pattern. This is the cloth of creative power.

A New Way   The vital Self, which you are discovering now deep within 15 your heart, is unburdened. It is light and all-intelligence. When you align and accept that person who you are, you are at peace, and nothing but peace can be with you.

Center yourself. Live in Me, not in the world. Keep the 16 focus on the Christ. Every activity should be of Me now. Let go of all sense of self. Personal life fades away as you open to a new way. Release all negative thoughts about yourself and lift your thoughts to what you truly are: a light divine. And cast no doubt out upon the waters of your life.

Look to the Father-Mother God, the Light nesting within 17 your heart. Be there with Me. Then express out of yourself *I AM,* the born-again spiritual energy field that is you and I as integrated light. Then say with the Master Jesus, "I and *my* Father are one." (John 10:30)

Blessed are they who understand this truth: I have created 18 man in the image and likeness of God. I have registered Man in Me as the Son of Myself, all glorious and supreme. I have then established Myself to be with him[2] always as the universal substance of all life.

Man (consciousness) is divinely ordained to rise to the divine 19 idea I AM. Man is good; he/she is of the Sun, light of My Being. He/she is not separate from Me. He/she has always been and ever shall be Myself. I AM aware of this but I want Man to be aware of this also. Man is My declared expression.

---

[2] Or her.

Ask and you shall receive. Knock and I shall answer. Live in My Presence only. I will fill you with My Being.

✧ Start the day in the Presence. Release the rhythm of 20 divine life who I AM.

✧ Step into the rhythm of Be-ing. And live each moment 21 in this perfect rhythm of Be-ing. It is always joyous and is ever creative and loving.

✧ Dance the dance universal in the vibration of I AM. 22 Open and Be. For I AM your abundant life. Enter Me and live joyously in love and light. We are one.

Homework

1) Do you have the same situation or experience reoccurring in your life? Over and over? Repeating itself? If so, describe this in your journal or notebook, then look at it objectively.

2) What is the lesson? What is your inner self, your GodSelf, telling you? What is the message? Are you blocking new thought?

3) *Be still and know that I AM God.* Let the "I AM" within you reveal why this lesson has been repeated and what you are to learn from it. Trust. Put your hand in God's Hand. *Listen.* Your world may shake but I AM here, with you.

4) Look at the reoccurring situation as you have written it down in your notebook. Look at it. See *its nothingness.* There is nothing to be afraid of here.

5) In a receptive and a meditative state, receive God's Voice in you. Hear His love, His absolution through you as you open your heart and truly *receive.* Every muscle and fiber, every bone and tissue of your body is in a *receptive state* now. Be at peace. Be receptive to the Christ Truth within you. Your receptivity will open the door to the divine teacher.

6) In this open and receptive state, let go and let God. Divine Mind will show you why this repetition has occurred.

7) You function in Spirit now. Record in your journal the thoughts and the ideas that come to you. You are building up a *receptivity* to God's Voice (the Christ within).

8) You may feel that you would like to have an affirmation as a way to dissolve the appearance/the difficulty. That affirmation of Truth will come. Write it in your journal, for you will be using it often as a powerful implement, a tool, for the subconscious mind.

9) Open in faith. Let Truth reveal Itself. As It does so, blockage dissolves and attachments drop away. A quiet peace settles in: *I AM.* And all that *is and ever was* is revealed in the quiet place of this "I AM." Here does the master dwell.

10) Let the process of fulfillment continue to work through you as Divine Mind cleanses and reveals your true being to you, the ever present GodSelf.

CHAPTER ELEVEN

The Moment Is Perfect

As you learn to grasp the moment in Me   1
—I AM ever fresh in the now—
so you can live without the human concepts
that have bound you. You are set free.

As human belief structure collapses a new one rises up: 2
that of My Being as Truth in realized form. You are My
idea, My thought form and My original creation. *I want to
know Myself as you,* I want to know My Son's Life in you.
That is My intent. *I come to know you.*

I would release you of all karma if you would stand in Me 3
as one with Me. Conscious of My will in you as My own, My
life has no karma. What I AM is all there is. There is no other.
I AM that which is given and that which is centered in Me as
I AM. All else is but illusion. I AM the life of Myself in
expression now. I AM THAT I AM: God in expression in this
moment. I have no past nor future. Look unto Me and I will
express. Stand with Me and declare in harmony with My
nature: *I and my Father are one.*

Thus the day can proceed as activity of My Self. Let Me 4
live in you as perfect order and love. There is nothing to fear
in Me for I AM everything. Without Me no thing is. I have
created everything and placed everything in My order.

Come Into   Your day is your expression of God. A day is a unit of God. 5
The Day   It is the glorification of My Being. It is My breathing in and
out. It is oneness.

No day is greater than this day; no day holds for you more 6
promise. Live in the day, in each perfect moment. Never will

it be a better day. Reach into the perfection of Being and draw forth your day.

You are the activity of My Consciousness, remember that. 7
The Lord is the frequency of your day.

No Other Life Come into the Presence where life is perfect. Enter into 8
My day of Be-ing. I never left you but you must be conscious of Me, *know* that I AM with you always. Without that knowing, you are not conscious. You have yet to be born.

I AM conscious only of My divinity, and I have no other 9
life but this. Let not thoughts of rejection nor patterns of old ways confuse you. Perfection is.

I AM all you ever need. I AM the rebirth within you. 10
Everything is in order in Me. No need to battle with the old order, for the old order has been cast out by My Son who lives in Me as the I AM. In Me you have everlasting and ever present life. And there is peace.

Receive Me in the moment. Focus on who I AM right now. 11
You are sitting at the table with Jesus. That is how I view you. This is the placement of your energy in the greater part. Lift now to that energy field that is conscious of itself as the *I* of all existence. Who I AM cannot be separated from you. *Before Abraham was, I AM.*

The Great Seed Concentrate on the real and let the personality of the "little 12
self" go. Relax into the immortal Self you are in Truth. You are Be-ing, expressing the Omnipresence of God as I AM. Release all that is not of Me. This will bless you, the "you" of Me, in many ways. What does it matter who you were or where you are going if I AM? All power is in God who rests within your immortal soul. Be free in Me!

God in you is as a Child (a Seed) asleep until realization 13
dawns of who you really are in Truth. Then personality or the "little self" drops away to reveal the Light of the World, the divine Self, God *within you*. Immanuel. God reveals Himself

through you as the radiance of Being. Such a Child was born to Mary, Soul of Man, in Bethlehem.

When you constantly look back and reclaim the past, you 14 are drawn into misconceptions of the Self. You forget who you are. Your growth will be stunted on the plane of conscious awareness. When you live with Spirit, you will know Spirit as your Self. *Be conscious of who you are.*

Forget the Old Testament. Let it be forgotten. It is the old 15 order. There is no truth there. There is a *new* order that has proclaimed itself through Jesus the Christ and this new order is the Presence of God vibrating through you. *I AM!* The Christ Truth is everywhere if you would but see it.

You cannot be as I AM and hold to the old, the false and 16 the untrue. As you identify with the old patterns and relationships, I drop away from you. Weakness is drawn back into your system. You are powerless to proclaim the light.

You cannot have one foot in and one foot out. In order for 17 Me to know Myself in you as I, both feet must be anchored firmly in My Kingdom. You are then not subject to the vibrations of the old patterns. That is why I say: There is no karma in Christ. These things are given that you might rise into the welcome arms of My Being. I long to embrace you as My Self.

No Man Need Look Back

Begin your new life by the recognition of the Christ in 18 you, the GodSelf. You have the perfection of My being resting within your heart and I AM ready to express. Will you have My perfection in you as I AM?

Your life is *new* in Me. Once you enter the Kingdom of 19 God nothing of the old life exists. Nothing. You are in a whole new world of light and love. Only in this moment, *now,* can My Sun light the world. *To Be still and know that I AM God* means just that. Allow God to realize Himself in you. That is the stabilization key. In that moment of unity and perfect reliance on God within, you are as the Sun blessing all.

Christed by My creative power, in tune with My Being, blessed in My love. Nothing is expected of you but perfection. And I AM That.

The expression of God remains always alive in your soul 20 but you must realize and accept it. The power is there, but you must be willing. Seek Me out of yourself. I AM deep within. Waiting. Always waiting.

You function in love. Remain in the present, looking only 21 at the past when necessary through My eyes and heart. Then you will know forgiveness for everyone who has harmed you in any way.

No man need look back save to thank God for his or 22 her lessons in Truth. But remember, DO NOT REPEAT THE SAME MISTAKES AGAIN! Once is enough. Let go and let Me live. I AM the presence of light. I AM your Self. To forget the past means to receive what is *presently* active *as the new creative process* in your heart. In this way every moment is perfect and original in its conception. I AM you.

Let your thought be harmonious with My Spirit. Let us be 23 creative together. Exact rhythm of Me is found in the present reality where I AM. This constitutes the creativity of the moment—the *now.*

Remember Stand in the reality of this moment, not in the regions of 24 the dead.

Raise your thoughts to the creative Presence, the vital 25 Presence. Interacting with that Presence, receive the brilliance of new worlds and rhythms of new being. Radiate brilliance into your workplace. Let Me give you fresh new ideas. Creative Intelligence. *Be.*

In the holy spheres of light where I AM, the Breath does 26 the work. The Holy Breath is the "do-er." Come enter the Breath, or Presence of God, where I AM. Receive My brilliance and legions of light will be with you.

Live in the moment—in the Creator—as divine love. Then 27
the Universe will serve you. When the Universe is with you,
you will have no poverty.

I Reveal   The Creative Energy always registers in the final hour. 28
The One   Remain conscious of your spiritual energy at all times. This
governs the universe, the planet, your own life expressing.

Let your thoughts be on Me. There is no hereafter. Only 29
now. Creation stems from this.

Seek that which is for *this* hour. Seek that which is given 30
for this moment. Each moment is fulfilled in itself as I AM.

You serve spontaneously now in the Christ. Release the 31
past and enter the Presence where I AM. Let the dance begin!

You Have   Rejoice, for the Word (Seed of all creation and creativity) is 32
Command   with you. Let the Word form of Itself, and speak with the
Energy that is contacted within the Word. It is the
Omnipresence of God reinstating Itself throughout creation.

It is not necessary to memorize a decree. The decree is *I* 33
AM: God Consciousness reinstating Itself as Be-ing. I want
you conscious of Me in all ways. I come as decree!

I AM the Word. Listen. Can you not hear My decree in 34
you? As you learn to look to the Oneness in spontaneous
union, I speak in glory as the Word. *And I will not have it*
broken.

Be centered in Me. Watch and wait. In Me is Thought 35
concentrated and divine. One Word from the Father suffices.
The divine decree is I AM. Have no gods before Me. You
build false images if you do. Leave behind ritual and be God
centered. Be not fearful in this: I AM the power and I rule
My Kingdom well!

Look Not To   Please live in the moment. *Make no plans for tomorrow.* To 36
The Future   activate the present, you must *be* there. All your attention
must go to that place. This is the "I AM," the Creator in you

as you. I stand with you in the moment as Divine Creator and Universal Life Force. When you move and have your being in Me there is no trial nor crucifixion. There is only one Be-ing. I AM That! Center in the GodSelf of Be-ing.

Look not to the future for I AM all there is. When I AM 37 the ALL in your conscious realization, you are stabilized in Me and *there is no other.* Inquire not into your future. All is well in Me. The world is governed by Me, the sacred life force I AM.

CHAPTER TWELVE

All Is Good

In knowing that you are with Me, 1
what can befall you but divine Good?
The key to relationships is in this statement.
Pay attention to this, for it is important.

Are you not ready to abide in Me forevermore *as one and* 2
the same? Be united with Me in My harbor of
contentment. Each day is perfect in Me.

Stand ready to see Me in all things. Drop the illusionary 3
consciousness that has had you stalemated. When you know
Me you see the perfection of all life. It is the *agreement* with
Me that changes your reality.

Come, live in the Presence that simply knows Itself in you 4
as I AM. The Thought Adjuster[1] does the rest. I embody
through your thought, through the creative power that rises
within that thought.

I created you out of Myself—out of My Son's Life in Me— 5
as perfect, divine and wonderful. I AM not separate from
you; I have come that you might know Me.

I AM you. 6

Come Home Until you see the reality, you are struggling to perfect 7
something that is not.

It is not necessary to change discord or the false picture, 8
for that which you see is not real. I have no part of it in Me.
In My eyes it does not exist, it has neither part nor place. I
give no thought to it. It is not of My Body and therefore
cannot be.

---

[1] The Father fragment or Spirit.

Let the flow of My eternal Breath be in you. Allow that 9
Christ light to shine through the open heart and see no evil.
Behold the Christ as I AM!

The revelation of creation is in Me. I stir the saplings of 10
My new creation. I release tension from your body. Oh, how
helplessly you flounder until I AM there as your risen awareness
and wondrous Self. When I know My Son's life as you, then
divinity is personified. I AM that which is the life of your
being.

Go forth in the day to reveal Me, unfolding as the Light of 11
God through all nature: in tune with all life, in perfect rhythm
of My being. As you walk creatively, looking to the Christ
within to objectify in all your life experiences, negativity will
cease to be.

Original Creation   *Go back to the beginning where I AM.* Remember, do not 12
try to correct past mistakes but go back to the beginning
where I imaged you out of Me as the I AM. As you know Me,
so you will know yourself and live in peace.

There are no limitations in the perfect order of man,[2] the 13
Order of Melchizedek. Remain in the One, who I AM, where
all harmony exists. Listen to the Light within weaving its web
of unity and creative intent. I AM within you as the Creator.
My land is yours. Let Me *think.*

I AM free of all past records. No karma (the law of cause 14
and effect) washes over Me, for I AM Truth itself. Therefore
do not look back. You dissipate the energy when you do this.
Look within and seek the God light as your answer. *I AM the
truth and the life.*

The more you look to "past lives," the more you become 15
encumbered by the laws of material existence. MY LIFE IN
YOU IS NOT ENCUMBERED! There are no past lives in
Me! I AM *beyond* reincarnation! I AM not earthbound. I live

---

[2] "Man" as it is used here means consciousness. The Order of Melchizedek is the order of
perfect man or consciousness. It is the GodSelf.

in the Presence and I AM THAT I AM. I AM fresh, I AM new Omnipresent Life in action now!

The only true life is I AM. This moment. Now! I have 16 never been born nor shall I die. *I AM*. The glorious return to Christ Consciousness enables full Truth to shine forth as a living light for all creation. Illusion vanishes and has its place in you no more.

Your consciousness in agreement with Me is "I AM." From 17 this point on, the High Self is Law; you are the Creator in creation as I AM, the Word made flesh.

Let In Love   *God is love.* (I John 4:8) Relax in Me. Your true nature is 18 divine love.

As you express as love you are at peace. My nature is rising 19 in you. Once stabilized in God you cannot punish yourself nor anybody else. The root of all punishment stems from self-hate. How great is My love! How abundant!

Come Home, My children, to the very place I have prepared 20 for the children of light, My anointed seed of Me. I have prepared a table for you. It has all things you could possibly need upon it. Will you sit with Me?

CHAPTER THIRTEEN

Forgiveness

The Universal Christ knows only love.   1
My true nature is love.

As Christ, I AM all-forgiving: 2
unceasing and unending love.

L earn to forgive yourself rapidly. When you dwell on your   3
faults they will multiply. Return to the GodSelf and focus
your attention on Truth. I AM there. Give your full attention
to Me. As you focus on Me I will expand in your consciousness.
I will begin to think and have My Being through you. Let Me
be who I truly am: your Christ Self. Be clothed in Spirit. Now!

Forget the past. You have entered into a new rhythm and a   4
new life where error has no place in you. *Fear not, it is I.*

As you release the past, believe in Me. Whatever you let go   5
of will be gone if you really mean it! There is no turning
back. Let go and come home to the universal Presence I AM.
Here AM I.

Forgive yourself and do not hold yourself in condemnation.   6
That hurts and denies the Christ Light within you. Take your
focus off the "devil," negative appearances, and focus instead
on God's presence within your heart. Dwell in that reality.
Light will come. Balance will be met. It is your destiny to
walk with God. In Me you have no enemy.

Free yourself by freeing others.   7

Enter My   In the blackest moment, you have Me with you. I AM   8
Being   creative supply. I AM not a punishing God nor do I hold

grudges, memories or thoughts against My creation. Only you can do this. I have only love in My system. My circuits express love. Hug this God to you. It is truth.

I know only perfection. The Seed of Christ risen in you is 9 that perfection. Know that you can only punish yourself by constantly referring back to that which has no part of My Son's Life in you. Let go. I want you with Me. Therefore, forgive yourself. Claim the understanding of My Law in your heart. All you have to do is to be willing and let Me go about My business. My business is *you*.

Cling not to old ways. Feel the loving Consciousness of 10 God within you. Take your place in Me. Become vitalized by Me and renewed. Let Me be. My child, whatever your mistakes have been, whatever the sins, let My loving Heart bathe you and cleanse you of anything unlike Myself. I AM original creation. I AM you. Have the power to take up your new life. This is the resurrection. Behold I AM you!

Forgiveness is part of God's love. Do not hold to any past 11 mistakes other than to learn from them. You are requalified in love, remember that. From love you can take your first steps as a new person. Enter God's Heart now. It is heaven on earth. I want to love through you and give everyone My forgiveness. I AM the Christ in you.

You may have suffered much, but now you are awakened. 12 Be joyous in the springtime of your life. Forgive and forget; live in the presence of God's world, the world of light where abundance flows.

Keep a peaceful pattern of love in your heart *and forgive* 13 *all*. Open every pore and every molecule to the giving Spirit of love that is now activated through your system. Then your peace will come. To know God is to know peace.

Brothers All   Forgive those who have hurt you in the past and they shall 14 be transformed in your eyes, for is not everybody of Me in reality?

Forgiveness is very important. Hold no grudges. Give to 15 the Father-Mother God any grievances you might have. Let them go. Forget and forgive. What you hold on to with bitterness and resentment will follow you through life after life. There is good reason for you to forgive. Until you do you are a prisoner in your own attachment.

As you give to God all your grievances *with the desire to* 16 *forgive* anyone and everyone who may have caused you pain and suffering, so God can transform this suffering into light! By your releasing to God all your hatreds, bitterness, resentments, God can then release through you His Christ love! *Until this takes place you cannot truly enter the Kingdom of heaven nor realize your fruitfulness thereof.*

As you forgive others, so you are also forgiving yourself. 17 An ocean of love covers you, washing clean the past afflictions. If you nourish bitterness, you hurt yourself. Lack of forgiveness may result in illness of the body and the mind. It hardens and causes illness, pain and even death. Practice instant forgiveness! It is good medicine. You say, "But I have tried and I cannot forgive." That is all right. Call on My spirit of forgiveness and allow My Christ Love to flow through you, and wash clean the roots of false creation.

What you forgive will come back to you as love. And you 18 will be blessed sevenfold.

CHAPTER FOURTEEN

Letting Go

Let the joy of God be with you: 1
His love and grace.

Always remember to let go.   2
Allow yourself to be lifted into the clean air of My Spirit.

I lift you in My Presence to the fullness of Be-ing   3
and I radiate My Self-expression out
as Word of God, the Divine Intelligence I AM.

It is the belief in your innermost Self that does the 4
work: the Creator within your own heart and mind.
The Creator functions as your *creative power* (We are one
and the same) once your heart has been opened.

Every heart has a mortal shell that must be broken. 5
Once that outer shell is broken, the Christ vibration
shines forth and does the work through you, dissolving
all error in your system. *I go before you making straight
the way.*

**Bear
Witness
To Me**

If you believe in blockages, they will be there; if you 6
believe in problems, they will be there; if you believe
in obstacles, they will be there. Yet, if you understand
My reality, which is the Christ within you, the purging
of all these things not of My life will automatically
take place in joy, in love.

Know that in God there are no blockages, no faults, no 7
disagreements. We come together in perfect order to express
together divine love.

There is only one life, therefore there are no 8
obstacles. Give no power to that which is not of
Me. Let the truth unfold, and it will.

It is in the letting go that I can remove all obstacles from your 9
mind. Let your consciousness rest in My Consciousness. It
doesn't matter what has gone before. The measurement
of My Consciousness is so great that it consumes all else.
Illusion vanishes.

Fear Not The GodSelf knows no fear. Loose and let go. All illusion 10
will vanish in the creative power of My rhythm and My way.
Do not be frightened, My child. I send illusion packing! The
Father-Mother cares for the only Son. That Son is your Christ
Self, the living expression of God in you. As you center on
that divinity within your soul, the Father-Mother *gives*. And
the measure of My giving is without end.

You don't have to ask. Divine Mind *knows* in the perfect 11
rhythm of creation. How does God Mind know? The Mind
of God knows because that mind is *your* mind as you accept
your Christ Self, the indwelling GodSelf.

Breathe in the light I AM. Then let Christ within your 12
heart dissolve that which has caused you pain and confusion.
Shine forth the new Consciousness of the soul. Be healed by
the light. As the divine Power of Life and Love embraces
you, all subconscious blocks leave. You are aligned in Me.
The Christ Force is set in motion through your heart and
soul.

Know that I AM the center of your being. I AM One, 13
whole and complete. There is no other. When you seek
balance, seek God. With this consciousness, you cannot fail.

As the creative power rises, it will light your body and your 14
mind. Your body may feel rushes of this fire-like increased
energy. There will be increased power in your brain centers as
well. At this time stand positive and *trust* in the Light within.

Put all your faith in that place. Energy rising in the understanding *I AM* strips away all illusion. Your karmic package drops away. The veil is lifted.

As you release all sense of separation, the subconscious clears 15 and becomes the superconscious mind. Now the way is open to understand truth and reclaim your inheritance. You must walk bravely though, for many will question your sanity, even those who have been close friends.

Transcending The Appearance Once you have cleared any blockage that you may have 16 discovered within your unconscious, more will materialize until you realize *I have no blocks in Me!* This self-realization creates the power level you need to transcend the appearance and vibrate wholeness and purity.

Inner light dissolves subconscious blocks. These things are 17 dissolved by light. Thus positioning yourself—knowing your identity in the GodSelf—establishes you in the light frequency of My Son. *I know Him:* the perfection of be-ing, the "I AM." I know no other.

Wherever I AM, you are there too. Because we cannot be 18 separated. This is an important statement which gives a whole new realization of identity. You may not understand this yet, but you will. *Take now the perfection of your being and be one with it.*

✧ Align consciously with the depths of your being, the 19 I AM expression, the infinite Light of the One who harmonizes with all life in perfect accord. There is no division in Me.

✧ As you accept and decree this Life as your life and 20 consciously agree with God as Being, the Life Center itself will activate and become the Self-governing process through your system.

✧ Then all else not of the creative process must drop 21 away. This is because you have withdrawn the energy or power from the problem, the false, the untrue, and *given* the power to God within your own consciousness. *You have become a Melchizedek!*

✧ In the context of energy, you have solidified your 22 energy and formed a vibration of permanent command. You are the Christ Center in Me. What your consciousness relates to and agrees with, is. I AM whole and complete in you. I have never left you but you must know this.

The Spirit purges and throws off what is not of Christ, 23 the image and likeness of Truth. What is Truth remains. What is not of Truth must drop away. This is LAW.

Do not...and I repeat...DO NOT try to hold onto or claim 24 back that which is already released by the Spirit. There could be serious consequences. Remember you cannot have one foot in the world of illusion and one foot out. You cannot compromise the lie.

Your new identity is waiting for you. Claim that. Let your 25 recognition be with My Spirit that the Spirit I AM may clothe you with immortal *light*. This is initiation. The "new" creation is a new world of expression. Enter the world of light. The atomic field is open to you now.

CHAPTER FIFTEEN

To See Anew

The Light of God has already ascended.　　　　　　　　　1
Come follow Me.

I have transcended all darkness in you. Align with Me.　　2
I AM the light within you. I AM the way, the truth and the life.
Come into this vibration of true being and live eternally.

The only death you need be concerned with is the death　3
to the "little self." That is the only death needed. Once
you release energy that has been confined for eons and return
that energy to the GodSelf where you can participate with it,
there is no death. *For death is no longer necessary.* You operate
out of the higher self where I AM life.

Let go and let God is the transcendent call! Give back unto　4
Me all that I AM. I AM your life, AM I not? When you and I
are one, we walk as one. My Spirit is your spirit. In God's
world you are the I AM. This Presence is the perfected divinity
of your being, it is the creative essence that is your place in
Me.

There is no death in Me. There can be no death in this life　5
for I AM all in all. And there is no other. Give up death. Make
no concessions to death. I AM life intended. Receive Me in
you as I AM. There is no turning back. My blood is your
blood. Have you not taken communion?

Remember your reality. *You are fulfilled.* This fulfillment is　6
beyond mortal mind. It is not of the world. Such a conscious
union cannot be explained. As you return home, I fulfill you.
Be anxious not. I AM all there is in truth, but you must
discover this. Awaken! This is conscious knowing.

I AM the central vortex of your being, but I have not been 7 recognized yet. When you recognize Me and realize I AM within you as your Being, all life changes for you. Can you believe this?

Enter Me

When you have been "reborn," you are in My life 8 consciously and can receive from Me as a "son of God." I have been bathing you in My light but you must realize it. You must be aware of My Being in you as I AM.

My Consciousness receives you back unto itself knowingly. 9 I become conscious of your being in Me. We are one. You are then in My hands and I take care of you. I wash the tears from your eyes. I mend your heart. You will not be called separate, but one with Me. Truly My Son or My Daughter, *of Me.* And I give you the power of Melchizedek.

I Behold You As My Own

You have the ability to create through your being and live 10 in prosperity. However there is a lesson here, as nothing belongs to you. *You are a caretaker of the expression of God in your life. All possessions must be returned to God as soon as you receive them.*

Nothing can be taken from you as all is in God. In oneness 11 you have all things that you need, yet you are not possessed by these things, nor can you be controlled. No one can control you as you give yourself to Me.

Nothing leaves you that is not replaced by something 12 greater, infinitely more fulfilling. There is no loss in God. When you know this you are at peace. Enter My life. In Me you have everything you need. I AM *everything.*

The Process

Weep no more. When the dam breaks and old hurts are 13 released, let them pass through you. Be done with them. Remorse and self-pity can only impede the release of old energies.

As you forgive and are forgiven you must let go of the 14
thought-energy and identify with the love of God. That is
the process of release. Release cannot come if you are still
identifying with the old thought forms of yesteryear. They
are not for you *now!* The beautiful life that you are must come
forth, and that is known as the "Second Coming." When you
identify with the true idea of Light, Light will externalize.
You will be one with it.

Often it is helpful to talk to someone who will not morally 15
judge as this cleansing process is taking place. This helps to
process the old out of your system. You should always
remember that the battle is not yours, that the spiritual process
is moving *in your behalf* to cleanse and to induce the Light of
God.

The Christ Light is your God awareness. In the vibration 16
of Truth, all else disappears. Feast on the Light. I dissolve all
negativity within My reach.

Be Anxious   Remember to forgive. Love that one as you would your 17
Not   dearest friend. *Have no enemy in Me.* If you cannot feel love,
ask for love. Ask that divine love fill you and express through
you. Ask that you be opened in the heart to love.

Do not suppress your unconscious desires. And do not fear 18
them. They are nothing. *I AM all there is and there is no other.*
The unconscious is a bed of illusion. Unconscious fears and
desires will flow to the surface that you can be conscious of
them. Once you are conscious of the false seeds of creation,
you can let them go. Dismiss them.

The quiet will come and the serenity. Let tension go. Learn 19
to relax in Me. Let Me do the work. Let go that I might Be.

Consciousness   Much of the pain that you may have been feeling is the 20
Will   overthrowing of the old attitudes, the breaking up and
Resurrect   dissolving of crystallization. My creative power rises now in
you shaking off the old *and there is no death.* You may feel a

nervous reaction to this power rising, as your centers align and become adjusted to the rhythm. The various reactions to the creative power or kundalini will pass as the Light becomes a part of your system *by your acceptance.*

Solid Is My Ground   Walk in Spirit on earth. Feel the ground beneath your feet. 21 And know that in Me you cannot lose your footing. I AM your foundation and your life. I have made My earth that I might stand upon it. And solid is My ground underfoot! When you have Me you are complete.

Thoughts To Remember

1) Remember not to look back. Bathe not in the waters of discontent. As you accept the living rhythm of your heart as the Christ, so does that Christ Spirit clear the way and make the path straight. Fear not. I sow My seed well. Do not look back lest the cobwebs reach out and claim you once again. When you look back and return to old situations or patterns, you chain yourself to the old program.

2) Have you any idea who you are in Me? *I AM life.* Come closer to Me. Harmony only exists in My perfection. I come through you as perfection. Identify with Me, not with old patterns. Hold Me in your consciousness as the perfection of being. Know that I AM with you always. Then I can *Be.*

3) I formed you of Me. You are My perfect life. Each moment as My Consciousness is spontaneous, free and giving to the whole. As the attachments leave you, you are living in Truth as the divine Idea I AM. In such a way will I govern this earth through you. With this embodiment comes the Christ, the Priesthood of Melchizedek, universal love in motion.

4) All situations and experiences that have been a possible cause of bitterness are assets in the Christ dimension. Know that these things have been but steppingstones into higher consciousness. In this understanding you can let go of all hurt.

5) Stabilize. There is no cross of crucifixion in Me. I AM pure love ready to be harvested *through your love of others.* My gift is love.

6) I AM is your innermost Self, the true you. As you abide in Me you will be released of all karmic debt, be it good or bad. What you have to do is forgive and let go. Then I return to you consciously as God's world of light.

PART 2

Lifting the Veil

*The whole universe
is lifting the veil for you.
Be attentive!*

CHAPTER SIXTEEN

Free from Illusion

The only power in your life is God.　　　　　　　　1
I AM Omnipresent. All life at one.
In Me there is no other.
I AM the beginning and the end.

If you give anything power in your life, you have forgotten　2
Me. For AM I not all? There is no thing that is separate
and apart. I AM all in all. Experience My life through you.
My life runs through your veins. Thus you can say, I AM the
living temple of God. And I accept immortal life. In me God
lives and has His Be-ing.

You are the equivalent of "master" every time you speak　3
God's word in the rhythm of His perfect Be-ing. There is
harmony in Me. Listen! *There is no separation in reality.*

Contemplate Let's look at illusion. What is it? How can we best define　4
My Living it? *Illusion is the nothingness, that which has no foundation in*
Power In *the GodSelf.* God is omnipotent. In illusion there is no God.
You

As you turn inward to the vital action of Christ Truth,　5
illusion vanishes. It passes away. So it is with the out-picturing
of your mortal thought. Because I have not entered into your
thought and your desire, because you are not letting Me out-
picture, then that which you are experiencing and beholding
is rightfully called illusion. Yet bear this in mind: Your out-
picturing—without Me in it—*has no power.* And if it has no
power, it is not true. It is not of Me. IT HAS TO BE OF ME
TO BE REAL. *Here is your stabilization key. The Omnipresent
Life is the only authority.*

Therefore, do not try to heal or change the nothingness. 6
There is nothing there if you give up the picture! Believe not
in the illusion. Believe in Me. As the great metaphysician and
philosopher Emmet Fox has said: "Take your mind off the
problem and put it on God." This restabilizes you in Truth.
This is why I have urged you to forsake all else and follow
Me. For I know the way: I AM the truth and the life.
Remember, dear one, that which you have created out of
nothingness has no power. As soon as you release the picture
from your mind and stop believing in it, your world is righted
in Me. Where there is doubt I AM not.

Rejoice! I   Be aware that illusion is where I AM not. As you surrender 7
Would Bear into My loving arms and permit Me in you to finalize My
In You A   pattern, there will be no false appearances in your life. There
Son   is only one and I AM That. How glorious is your life in Me!
Come home.

The creative power rises up in you and bears the Son. The 8
Son or SUN is My inner glory. It is the light.

The light is as a Voice of unity and divine wisdom. It vibrates 9
as the keys of Enoch, and the holy matrix of Christed energy.
As you hear this "Inner Voice" as oneness with God or Truth,
you will know. This knowing is the Creator in you as I AM.
With this Voice you can command the heavens. Bear this in
mind as you open into My life. All that I have is thine. God is.
I AM the life-center of your being, the very breath that you
breathe. *Hear Me in you.* I AM the Creator fire. I AM That
which is within you as I AM.

There is only one power. Blessed are you with the radiance 10
of My Be-ing. I AM blessed with you. Together we are One,
a complete radiation. When I stand *with* you, we are One.

I AM the supreme Being that you seek within yourself. 11
You search everywhere but within yourself. Now look within.
Let Me live in you as I AM, your conscious experience
of God.

Changing Of Dimension

The Son of God is your consciousness. In this you move 12 and have your being. You are fully prepared to accept this now, for I have prepared you through Jesus. He is the blueprint and the passageway into the new world.

Take your place in that mold of energy that I have created 13 as you. All laws of energy must adjust and correspond to the cosmic blueprint *of the Living Light.* When no adjustment is possible that law—which exists in the finite realm of earth and matter—*must be discarded.* It may no longer stand.

God is whole and must externalize as wholeness. The Body 14 of Christ is not separate units organizing themselves into one body. The Body of Christ is a new star system for the cosmos. It is wholeness as Be-ing expressing supremely and without division. IT IS AN ORDER OF MAN. You are created to abide in this dimension of the Creator Son. *This will be the triumphant entry of the new world and its creative energy of love and light,* and is the unique destiny of humanity on planet Earth.

You are of pioneer stock, sent forth into the God body, 15 into the regions of light. There you must discover new lands of divine oneness and creative potential.

Disturb not My Kingdom, for it is already one, but enter 16 in and perceive what is; thus will you glorify Father-Mother God, the Living Truth, and be My Son in all ways. You will see the Creator and His manifestations at one. The God body has connected into your Earth dimension and is now feeling Itself in all avenues of Its creative power. *It is recircuiting Itself.*

Stabilizing Grace

Unification is My divine Principle; it is My world. Stand 17 with Me, for I cannot forsake you. Stand with My Being. I AM released Consciousness on your planet Earth.

I AM the walk, the step, the word. I AM the anticipation 18 on the Breath. No thing is without Me. I AM everything that is. I AM realized consciousness in you. I AM the day that is met; the full creation is My Word. I live in all life as I AM. My essence covers the globe like a blanket of divine Presence. I know and I AM.

We are walking together, you and I, in the wholeness. The 19 consciousness of Jesus made it so. As he gave himself as the Son of God, original creation, into human awareness, he became you and you became him. You have become a new circuit of Life intended! You are as one being in My thought and My world. Thus I know you as My Son. You are in Me and I AM in you. Together we are One. Enter that place that is provided in the rhythm of Jesus that you might live and have your being in the wholeness of the I AM.

The one you call Jesus (the master within you as you) 20 released certain energy lines of forgiveness and divine love that enabled Earth to rise into her new body as the radiant Sun she is. He, as Son of God, sanctified this heavenly planet and fulfilled *My need* to embody Myself as all I AM.

Divine Authority   Are you empty? I will fill you. Are you tired? I will give 21 you rest.

You are a vessel of My Consciousness, yet not separate from 22 Me. We are One. This Oneness is declaring Itself through your system as a planetary Christed body. Every cell is anointed by My light. Every tiny molecule. I AM with everything. In all life, I AM one.

You would be wise to listen to My Voice. I AM within you 23 as the "Inner Voice." Can you hear Me? Desire to hear Me as the Voice within: the Voice of counsel, direction and revelation. I impart wisdom to you. Heed My Voice when you hear it. Listen to Me as I counsel you and give you light. I AM the thread that unites all life, the living candle that cannot be put out.

When you hold Me in unity with all life, you will meet Me 24 in all creation. God speaks to you in many ways, through life itself. So listen, and God awareness will come to you as knowing.

My purpose is to enlighten you. Let the all-life become the 25 one life in your consciousness *as your consciousness.* We are one. You cannot live without Me. There is no life without Me.

Everything is in order in Me. Return "home." Then you 26 will be fulfilled. When you are conscious of Me only, you have entered the Kingdom and divine love is at your beck and call. Love is oneness, a unity with all life.

I harbor no shame. I AM the triumphant entry of *new* life. 27 I AM the registered authority throughout your system. I AM the Coordinator, the Giver, the Purifier. Look to Me and give Me power in your life. Then the mighty Seed will open and raise the curtain on your immortal life.

Nourish Me within yourself as the living spring of water 28 ever present. I have much to give you if you would but seek Me. I AM the Presence within you. I want to live, I want to be, *as you.* Together, at one, we are the order of divine oneness, the authority on this planet, the magnetic ray of Be-ing. Let us stand together, you and I, and live.

You Are The Vessel Of My Consciousness Praise God and illusion vanishes. God has no place in 29 illusion. I AM not there. There is one embodiment: I AM that. Sing the praises of your Lord who abides in you as your Be-ing. Then cut all ties other than this. Come home. The "home" is the Creator in you as your life. As you adjust to the frequency of My Be-ing, you are home. It is the position of your Presence in you as I AM.

Be not fearful of the illusion. Take command in the nature 30 of your true self who I AM. *The Lord is with you.* I AM come that *you* might Be. So let it be known that you are with Me and I with you. Together we are met as Son of God, rhythm of perfection. In unity we stand as life itself: the true embodiment of Christ Jesus who gave up his body that he might release you and fulfill his divine mission of Christ radiation in you and through you. Let the Christ live in you as the Son of God, the presence of your divine Self.

No matter what might seem to be, there is never a moment 31 that I AM not in command. I AM one with you and all life. As you forgive all those who may have hurt you and ask their forgiveness of you, you are lifted entirely out of the mortal world. The very act of forgiveness dismisses all previous records and returns you to your GodSelf, the I AM presence. Forgive daily and never let one thought of hatred or bitterness linger in your heart. As you release all into My world of light and love, I AM. Determine now who you are and bring that determination into reality.

CHAPTER SEVENTEEN

Look to Me

Remember to look to Me...   1
not to job, nor man.
Let your consciousness unfold.

My sheep know My Voice.[1] I AM the Consciousness within   2
them calling. My sheep are formed of Me. I AM stabilized
in them and they in Me. We are one. As it is, so it shall
ever be.

I shall call you out of "normality" and "conformity." I shall   3
be lifting you as the Light I AM. Now surrender all memories
that you might remember Me, for I AM not in the "past
life." I AM in the present. Find Me in the now. My Presence
is always personified in the now. I AM not in the past. These
things have been called to your attention so that you do not
fall back or lag behind. The temptation to linger in past
memories whether "good" or "bad" is great upon this planet.
You have clothed yourself in false doctrine and still do this
under the guise of a "new age."

Yes, I say to you: Be in My Spirit. Look not backward nor   4
forward. Be still and know, for I have come that you might
know. *I AM full knowing.* In the stillness, yea the quiet of
your heart, I will come to you. I will teach and I will supply.

Look Not To   In the world you meet with the false appearance, the human   5
The World   suggestion. Therefore, test the spirits! Remember Me and
call upon Me to enter your thoughts. I will then correct your
vision and clear your mind. Test the spirits and come to Me.
Where I AM there is no other and each day is of Me. The
false appearance dissolves in the light of Omnipresent God.

---

[1] See John 10:4.

Look not to the outer, what you see with finite eyes, but 6
always seek Me within and then consciously align with My
Spirit as creative energy. Then, and only then, balance will
come to your life. You will be in tune with the rhythms of the
Universe. Correct the imbalance you see in the world by
receiving Me—the living expression I AM—into your system.
Believe in Me. Let Me express outwardly. Look to Me as I
express. I AM perfect expression in your life. When you are
consciously free, you free others by your light.

Place your consciousness in My Consciousness. Dwell not 7
on the unreal, for the unreal has no power in Me. Give up
daydreams, those flimsy yearnings of the lower self. Have
majesty. Dream the true dream—that of the world of light!
And consciously affirm the truth of being.

True vision has substance, has power. It comes 8
by the Holy Spirit. It is omnipresent.

As you release the often selfish and lust-filled dreams of the 9
lower self, so will you rise to that place of the eternal vision
and there work with the creative process of your highest good.
The power of this is unimaginable. It may seem impossible
for your life intended to hold such promise, to be so good.
Yet you are raised to this promise and governed by this good.

How comfortable are you? How much can you give up 10
to attain this majesty of person, this glory of the soul? In
you is the way. In this positive consciousness you can dwell
on earth in peace and love. It is here in this God Consciousness
that you will find peace. Not in the world that you have made
or wish to make, but in My world: the vibrating world of
light.

I Wait   How do you look past the illusion to the reality or 11
perfection? In the moment that you seek, I AM there. I hear
you. I wait for you to seek Me. *The moment you seek Me I AM!*

What you see as "the world" is not real. Only I AM. I AM 12 the Creator in life. I AM the texture of the life I make and I say I AM good. Come to Me. Let the flowing river of My Consciousness be externalized through your heart and mind. I AM the true reality.

When you are in trouble, come to Me. When you encounter 13 an obstacle, turn from the obstacle to Me. I will remember you in Me and as I do, all dross is consumed by My love. As you receive Me in yourself, I must be. I rekindle My light in you.

You have appeared to have wandered, yet I have kept My 14 eye on you. I have let you wander that you might decide to return home to the Christ Self you are. I AM closer than breathing. In truth I have never left you. I wait for you to seek My Spirit in you. Then I come and settle into your heart and mind.

Recall I said, "Have no other gods before me." (Exodus 15 20:3) I fade from memory as illusion gains power in your mind. Yet always in truth I AM. Ever present. Never failing you. Always there...if you would but see Me and call to Me to come.

A Few Words Of Glory

❖ Stake your claim! As you learn to look beyond the 16 appearance to the glory of My revealed power, you are truly living the Christ Life as the Creator Son.

❖ Conscious union with the Christ Self dissolves illusion. 17 Realize that as you look to the higher self and reveal it, all else must pass away. Illusion has no substance in Me.

❖ Enter into Me, for I AM All Things. Come to that 18 place within your own heart where I AM.

❖ Keep your eye on the single spark of union within 19 your soul, that I might be born in all life through you. Look not to the appearance, but to Me. I AM ever present. You are never without Me.

✥ As you ask a question, know that I have an answer for 20
you. *Ask and you shall receive. As you seek, so shall you
find.* Look to the Christ within, for the world does
not have the answer. As you learn to live in the
Presence, so the Presence reveals Itself as truth.

✥ Draw on the inner wisdom that is your right as child 21
of God. You have infinite wisdom to draw from; you
need only to trust and let Me reveal. I have many
things I want to reveal and I will, *as you let Me.*

✥ When you take your eyes from the appearance and 22
look within your own heart and mind, you find the
great and mighty counselor. This Counselor is your
friend, one who connects you to the higher spheres
of knowing.

✥ When you give power to something other than God 23
in you, *you forfeit the immediate power I AM.* I AM
with you as your life. I acknowledge Myself as your
life. But you must believe. Then we are truly one.

I AM All   I AM the Image and Likeness of My Father's love for all 24
creation. And I have come that you might be lifted in
consciousness as *I.*

Empty yourself that I might be. The "I" is the true you. *I* 25
would have you blessed with My being. When you hunger, turn
inward to the Light. Foolish mortals give themselves away to
any master. Have you given yourself away? Then take your
Self back. *Reclaim who you are.* Align with the light! Reclothe
yourself with the diamonds of My hills. If you look to Me
you will never be disappointed. And there will be a creative
purpose not experienced within the mortal life.

So tarry not: Reclothe yourself in love and live with passion 26
with the glory center shining forth as I AM. Have the majesty
to Be and in this rhythm live eternally with the full life I AM.
Rest in Me. Keep your focus on the I AM presence within
your heart.

Reclothe yourself with light. I AM the Christ, your divine 27
center expressing as your GodSelf. The Creative Power does
not express other than through Me. I AM the only authority.

Pin no hopes on the outer or illusory world. There is 28
nothing there for you. Leave the material world in
consciousness. I will take you into a new placement of unity
where I AM. Release the world of chaos. Make your home in
Me and live in God peace.

I promise you nothing of this world, for "I" have naught 29
to do with the appearance. My declaration is of a greater place.
Your atomic field is changing. You are more than you think.
Rest in Me. I AM the new world that you seek. I call My
children home. What you see is not real. I AM real, for I AM
all there is. There is no other.

**What You
Seek You
Will Find**

See not opposition but Truth. Always look to the peace 30
behind the appearance. I AM there.

The true union is *within* you. It is in the heart. When you 31
seek only that, I AM. That consciousness prevails. And when
you hunger, I will feed you.

Give not one thought to that which is not real, not one 32
thought. Take your eye off the appearance and put it on God
or the frequency I AM. Always seek that Life as expression.
Seek Me in all life. I AM there.

When you do this you are fed, clothed and abundant. I will 33
always prosper you in Me.

In the powerful reunion of God and man is the GodSelf. 34
This GodSelf is desiring to express fully and in all ways for the
perfection of God's Plan on earth.

He who seeks the GodSelf is fulfilled. It is My pleasure to 35
give you the Kingdom. The Kingdom of which I speak is the
Creative Power, released and abundantly yours. Peace on earth
comes with the creative power completely stabilized as I AM.
Be there with Me in that place. Deny Me not.

CHAPTER EIGHTEEN

I AM Rhythm
in Divine Love

God is always with you.   1
Look not to the illusion of matter
but to the truth of My Spirit.
Lift your consciousness to the greater part.

Hold My Spirit in you *as the light*. I AM one with the 2
heavens. I AM one with all things. And love is My bounty.
My treasure house is open for you.

Be not caught by the lower realms. Be not imprisoned by 3
thought patterns that have no reality. Concern yourself with
My Thought and I will give it to you *abundantly*. The thirst
for knowledge comes from Me. I cause you to thirst for Truth.
I AM the One who brings that desire to you. I AM the
Thought Adjuster in you. I AM the One who sends you God
thoughts, the thoughts filled with Christ Power. And I give
you these thoughts to use as I AM.

Stay in the Creator *consciously*. In the nature of glamour 4
and illusion lie both the chains of maya and hypnotic control.
Selfish desire and lust have no footage in Me. Look to Me
only. I will answer you. In Me, the Center of your divine Self,
is the almighty Kingdom of God where all Truth dwells. Go
there for everything you need *and I will come as your answer.*

**No Past
Life**

I qualify My own flesh. There is only one identity: the 5
Creator in you as you. You and I are one. *We are one.* Once
stabilized union has been reached you will consciously know
and agree with this statement.

78

There is no past life in Me. To be born again is to be born of 6
My Spirit. I have never been born and I will never die. In this
conscious awareness past lives dissolve in the knowing I AM.

Dissolve *There is only the life I AM.* You are released from the hypnotic 7
Phenomena pulls of the astral plane as you seek the Oneness of all life in
expression now. Be *willing* to recognize and see the purity of
Being in all life. My Consciousness pervades all.

Remember the word "astral" means temporal: that which 8
is of illusion, not fixed in its awareness of Christ Consciousness,
without grounding in Spirit. The astral plane is the fool's
playground and should be avoided at all costs. It is the plane
of phenomena, division and selfish desire. It is the plane of
disillusionment where the emotions—not under the command
of Christ but under command of the senses—can cause very
serious discord.

The astral plane is the plane of the trickster. This is the 9
plane where dangers reside, where impersonal, unconditional
love cannot dwell. There are many deceivers here. Waste no
time in phenomena. Go swiftly to the Light!

I have need of you in My place where God and Man are 10
one. I abide in you and you in Me. We are one. All energy
completes itself through unity of My Spirit. Have My way. I
sent My Son Jesus that you might know My love for you. It
was My intention to bring you home through him.

The astral plane dissolves in the constancy of My Flame. 11
Those who know Me know I AM. When the astral plane is
eliminated, the truth will fill the consciousness. You will know
Me as I AM. We will walk together, you and I, in the regions
of light.

Be In My My thought is all-encompassing, completely satisfying, and 12
World it reaches deep into your soul. The body and mind come
together as I send My thought to you. I AM registering My
own Being as My thought. This is enlightenment. It collects

you into itself to Be. We are One in sound and thought. God thought is Be-ing.

You are a child of God. Let illusion go. Be in My world. I 13 have a Kingdom waiting for you—a Kingdom of LIGHT! There are no worlds other than My Word. My Breath is upon you now. I cancel out all idea of a false creation.

You are of Me and I of you. I nourish you *by My own Breath*. 14 I counsel you. I give you the life of Me. Remain still in Me; let the stillness be and all things come to pass by this stillness of Divine Love. It is the Creator.

Remain still in Me. Seek not a mission of doing; that can 15 cause phenomena and has no place in you. Seek a mission of Be-ing. Herein is the way. This way will be called the alignment with your higher self, your true Self, the Self I AM. *Be-ing* draws forth the I AM expression, the God force.

I cannot express you within phenomena. I have no place 16 there. If you move through the phenomena or psychic plane *without halting*, I will be with you as the Light of your true Self. But if you should be tempted to play with phenomena, the false gods of creation, there are serious consequences. You may fall back and reverse your place in consciousness as well as take on greater illusion in the form of false entities, false idols and false masters. Remain alert and seek always the Christ within.

Walk with the light of God in all ways. I sent My Son as 17 *light*, as *Master*, that you might not fall again.

No Other Before Me   When you enter Me *consciously*, I become the Master in 18 you: the Omnipresent authority. I have dominion over all life and through all life. I stabilize. I resurrect. It is My Word that beckons unto you and My Creative Power that decrees. I AM *the new law* upon your system. Thus comes a system of government that takes precedence in your life.

I have come that I might rise in you. I do not intrude 19 Myself on you. I do not do this. I rest, I wait, I call, I beckon.

My Seed (in your unconscious) takes root as you leave your old life behind and come to Me. That means NO FALSE GODS, NO FALSE IDOLS and NO SPIRITS OTHER THAN MY SPIRITUAL SELF. I AM decreeing Me as your real life into existence. I AM perfect order of being in you. It is My Breath you breathe, My laughter you feel. I AM the Order of Melchizedek, order of the One, stabilized in motion.

Be ye therefore perfect, even as your Father which is in heaven 20 *is perfect.* (Matthew 5:48) THAT REMAINS MY COMMAND FOR YOU. To this day I utter it, and it is heard.

I AM the One who is sent, the perfect order of Be-ing in 21 expression now. I AM true expression of Godhood in you. I AM That which is given as perfection: Image and Likeness of God, the Christ. In Me you have your being.

Be not directed by spirits of the psychic plane. All power 22 stands on High to direct you. It is My government you seek. When you are hungry, I will feed you. I come that I might harvest My own. Therefore look to Me. When you thirst I will fill you.

Be always drawn to the highest that you might be a blessing 23 to others. Keep your spiritual energy *alive* in the creative power of God in you. There is only one true Voice in harmony with My Spirit. That is the Christ emanation, embodiment of all that I AM. Be there with that Light and go forth in My direction.

My Consciousness is the Word. You know My sound. It 24 clarifies Itself. It will never flatter nor build a false sense of pride. Words tell you nothing lest they carry My Spirit. I AM all there is. Humans must leave the lie and come home to Me.

No Place For Illusion   Only in Truth will you find Me. As long as the desire for 25 illusion, applause or glamour is in the heart, the traps of illusion will externalize. Truth lives in the Heart of the Master. It is the Christ-idea. Thus, there is much misfortune on earth. The Christ-idea is not alive in the heart. Some seek entertainment and want apparitions to appear before them. They are seeking phenomena.

Divine Consciousness has no agreement with the plane of 26 *phenomena.* It is in agreement with the wholeness of life. In the revelation of your Inner Voice as Christ Light changes are made in your environment. Your consciousness realigns itself *into the Will of the Creator.* Many changes come through this alignment, as Christ in you speaks as My Word in motion. Act as the Christ. Do not allow the worldly enticements of the psychic to pull you down. Be conscious of who you are. *Act as the Christ.*

Discernment And Discipline   Too many students have become confused because they 27 have joined too many spiritual schools with varying disciplines, rites and beliefs. It is best to stay with one alignment of spiritual discipline, rather than to jump hither and yon. Let your chosen path carry you through into God Consciousness and enlightenment. Trust the soul to lead you into the spiritual practice best for you.

Many are caught in astral phenomena. They are caught 28 and cannot pry themselves free. They know not how to shake loose the ties that bind them and cause them pain. Yet I say My Presence frees them all! *I remove the ties, I shake the chains loose. I free them all! I come that I might release you from that which has bound you.*

There are no traps in Me! I release and set free. I come that 29 I might free you in Me. I come that you might be lifted. I come that you might be resurrected. Lean not toward the psychic phenomena nor to the place of personal acclaim. Come to Me. I tear down the walls of the false world. I provide new dimensions of Being.

The Word of God manifests only to those who release their 30 psychic desires and ambitions. The GodSelf is the only self there is. Remember that. My Spirit prevails. You are blessed of My Being.

A Review

1) Reality is the out-picturing of God in your life and as your life. Allowing God to really live through you results in harmony and Christ love.

2) The only power in your life is God or Truth. Give God the power and the authority to express. It is in this way that you will be happy and creative.

3) God speaks to you in many ways, through life itself. So listen, and God awareness will come to you as knowing.

4) Praise God and illusion vanishes. When the heart is lifted in gratitude and love, there can be no foreboding nor sense of self. The life of God emerges.

5) Forgive daily and never let one thought of hatred or bitterness linger in your heart. This conscious practice realigns you to the Kingdom of God and the Personality of the Christ.

6) Where I AM there is no other and each day is of Me. The false appearance dissolves in the frequency of My Spirit.

7) See not opposition but Truth. Always look to the peace behind the appearance. I AM there.

8) You are a citizen of the Universe. And in Me you have your being.

9) To be born again is to release the mortal life and to take on the life of God in you as the "I AM." Prisoner no more, you light the world with My Presence.

10) *You are the Seed of Me.*

CHAPTER NINETEEN

The Divine Appearance

You change your environment by your consciousness. 1
You need not move to have your environment change.
Every new realization changes your environment.
Conscious realization always brings results.

As you rest in Truth, I AM your environment. I AM with 2
you expressing outwardly as your environment. I AM
externalizing as you express Me as your consciousness.
Lovingly and trustfully rest in Me. Behold I make all things
new! You imprison yourself by forgetting I AM. I AM within
all life. See Me there. Walk in the truth where I AM. Let the
light shine. I AM ever present. I AM with you. In Me all life
is glorified and abundant.

There is nothing impossible in God. There is no problem 3
too great or too small. Please remember that all things must
be met in Christed Consciousness, in the Father-Mother God.
That is what Jesus did. That is what you must do. I AM Spirit
intended through all life.

Bring your attitude into balance by restoring My light in 4
your heart. Know I AM there within you as the light of the
world. If you but see My light within your own heart and
acknowledge this light in all hearts, My world shall come to
pass, the world of light. Be with Me and I shall show Myself
to you. I AM the Living Light. In Me all things are perfect.

For you have the ability to change that which you see by your 5
belief in My light. You can cause changes in your life by One
centeredness. The only thing that is real is the I AM. It is
never too late to come home.

God Is Your Dwelling Place

Your consciousness is your environment. You may not 6 change your neighborhood but through your conscious awareness your neighborhood will be transformed. For the nature of your consciousness does the work. This is a cosmic law. Thus it is your attitude that makes the difference!

Touch your vibrating Christ Presence within your heart. 7 This is the Kingdom of God. I AM then your environment, your home, your surroundings. I AM all and everything in this place. When you operate out of Christ Consciousness, the Creative Power will rise as direct expression of light.

You are blessed to have the full God Trinity within you. 8 This is the true government on earth. When you know the Life Center within, your environment is of the light.

Therefore, stabilize not in the location, but in Me. As I 9 AM all there is in Truth. There is no other. Each day is perfect in Me. One day at a time.

God is your dwelling place, in Him you have your peace. 10 Your responsibility is to stay aligned to the God Presence within. Then, *I AM* in expression always. Focused upon the Christ within, you know the Kingdom of God and experience the indwelling Creator in expression.

Don't Limit Yourself

When you change, others change with you because your 11 vision has altered, hasn't it? What you see is your world, false or true. You inhabit the world of your making. Change your consciousness, you change your world. We are the makers of our own destiny, the creators of our own world. When you accept the light as yourself, you become the light, and the world is light. For you cannot be light without the world of your being also translating itself to light. That is the law.

You are the light of the world. So take thought on this and 12 move accordingly. When God gave "His only Begotten Son," He was decreeing out of Him-Herself a world of unity and world peace. Such a world you find in your own consciousness.

**Here Is
The
Kingdom**

The more you realize and recognize the Kingdom of God 13
within you, the more you can visibly see and experience what
the "Kingdom" means as your environment and your
surroundings. Might you say then: The peace that I seek is
within me as I AM. Come to that place within where you can
say this and know this.

Every atom—be it in a table, a chair, a blade of grass, a bird 14
that flies—every atom is touched and glorified by My radiance
through you! You must see Me to know this. Where AM I?
Within yourself. Stabilize there. Let Me be glorified.

As you permit God to express, your surroundings change, 15
electric circuits are rearranged, and a new vibration is qualified.
It is My own. Such a vibration can only be called "wonderful,"
the Christ life in you.

You do not have to move to change your surroundings, 16
because you enter a new dimension which activates new
vibration all around you. The denser atmosphere begins to
sparkle. It takes on new life. All molecular structure will
change, taking on greater life fire or life energy. Your love
from your innermost heart is transferred to your surroundings.
Density begins to sparkle and to take on tones of lightness
and reality.

You have the ability to change your life—if you *want* to. 17
The higher life or the spiritual side of your nature begins to
rearrange itself as your life. God becomes your body and your
mind. New thoughts come that are of the intensity of God
awareness. My God Center is open then. My light shines.

**Laughter
Comes
Easily From
The Heart**

The coming of the Kingdom is now. Harmony is vibrating 18
as the essence of the Kingdom. The environment responds to
the heaven within your heart and soul. Thus can you live in
peace. You have dominion, you know. You decide. When you
are at peace, your surroundings will be at peace also.

There is no heaven other than your own conscious 19
experience. Heaven is a state of mind, supremely given from

the heart of man. And the environment yearns to feel your resonance and light! God peace is to be given, bestowed on others.

You are releasing Truth from your GodSelf. And that Truth 20 must take form. So you see what a wonderful thing it is to recognize Truth from within yourself. Those who contact you feel the Presence and are warmed by your light. You are like the sun rekindled in the heart.

The GodSelf longs to show Itself. But It cannot without 21 your agreement. Only with your consent can I come forth and warm My earth and bring My peace of mind. I AM the house, the city, and your environment. I AM within you as the heart of God. I AM the Christ within. I AM waiting. Living in Me is the Creator in form. See Christ in all life. See Me and I will be-come. Here is the master key to life.

I move through the experience and change it. *I enter the* 22 *environment and qualify it through your conscious awareness of Me.* Didn't I say, I have meat that you know not of?[1]

As I guide you and try you and temper you, be aware that 23 I already know who you are, for I have claimed you as My GodSelf: the living idea of who I AM.

Lift your surroundings to Me where no error can claim 24 you. See Me through everything and everyone. Allow no environment, home or job to ensnare you, to capture you and control you. The supreme good that you seek is that which lies within yourself.

Be joyous and be fruitful. Live in the Presence, then all is 25 of Me. I reclaim My creation into Myself as I AM. Laugh and be not afraid. Seek only That which I AM. Then all is well. Bless My identity in you.

Appearances   The Christ Conscious individual dissolves all that is not of 26
Dissolve   peace and joy. Any and all obstacles that might appear are immediately dissolved and recreated no more. Any and all obstacles are met with joy and laughter by the one who knows

---

[1] See John 4:32.

I AM all and everything. Appearances are altered radically in the light of Truth awareness. The GodSelf does not know age, nor decay. You are mortal no longer in Me. I AM beyond age. I AM Be-ing. Life itself.

Look not to the past but *to the Presence I AM*. The I AM 27 Presence is your Self. As you stabilize in this awareness all truth comes naturally as the leaves on the tree. What is to be will be in the God Consciousness you are.

My Perfect Son On Earth   I have established you in this frequency that I might Be. 28 How many will believe upon this and understand?

As you learn to rely on Me, appearances dissolve. The 29 activity of My Consciousness removes the illusion. I AM the first and the last, the beginning and the end. I cover the earth and all of life with My Being. I AM you. Why do you answer any other call but this?

The translation of this Consciousness—this living fire of 30 Truth—into your life stream, completely accepted and completely realized by you, vibrates to all My creation. You are My Sun after the Order of Melchizedek. I recognize this and fill you with My light. *I AM the creative power in you as I AM returned.*

The Living Truth In You   Remember not to fight imperfection or illusion. Do not 31 set up an enemy! God's peace is here and now; give it embodiment through your trust and faith and all-knowing.

When you fight error, you will always give it power. 32 Error cannot stand when it is not recognized.

Do not get caught in the mesmerism of the false 33 appearance nor attempt to correct the appearance, *for it is not real of itself.* There is no reality other than the living truth I AM. Thus rest in the Spirit of God and let God objectify. Rest assured, God is! The appearance has no reality. Drop the appearance, the grand illusion. Let it go.

I AM all there is, and there is no other life but 34
My own. Correct nothing. Adjust nothing. I AM
perfect. And behold My perfection in others.
Wherever I AM there is perfection.

I AM The   Carry forth My form, My rhythm, on earth. *Light harvests* 35
Living Way *light.* The light from within you as you dissolves all difficulties,
cleanses and resurrects. I AM the light of the world, AM I
not? *Let the light so shine in you that I AM recognized and
loved.* I AM the rhythm and the life.

As you learn to lift Me up through all seeming appearances, 36
you ignite the Earth with new hope. Carry Me forth. Let Me
live in you! Let My light shine! Instead of trying to change
the environment, let the environment I AM be released
through your alignment. For in this way do you serve the
Master. Let Me rise in you as your conscious awareness. And
do not look back.

Recognize Me in you as I AM. You will feel My rhythm, 37
yes, My activity. I will pump new blood into you. My blood is
your vital force.

In this rhythm have your being and move in it. This rhythm 38
is called the way. It is the Order of Melchizedek, the flowing
energy of your spiritual life. You are opening into a river of
light and love, a constant expression of Melchizedek, the divine
being you are in Truth. In this consciousness you will stand
as the Christ, the light of the world. In Christ, you and I
are One.

CHAPTER TWENTY

Take a New Appearance

As your consciousness changes, so your appearance changes.   1
Consciousness is the substance of your reality.
As you live in the Presence, you are living in perfection
where no negativity can reach you.

Your outer appearance always is a reflection of your inner   2
growth. How do you appear to yourself? Do you see
love expressed through your eyes, the all-abiding love that is
the eternal vision? The love of the GodSelf for all creation?
Are you radiating Self-esteem as the Oneness of My Be-ing?
If you can answer these questions in the affirmative, you are
as one who carries and embodies the I AM Presence. You are
the GodSelf intended. The very Life I AM.

Now rise and shine. You are meant to be the Sun of God,   3
the brilliance of the GodSelf externalized. Realize this! You
are entitled to *Be*. When you embody the Christ Idea as you,
you are most certainly "well dressed." You are the divine idea
yourself.

When I open the records within you, I mean to live them   4
as you. Remember that. I come that I might be. So let Me
unlock the records within you. That you might know I AM.

When you allow negativity to govern you, when you allow   5
anyone or anything to govern you, you are not at one with
Me. I AM all there is. My intent is to show you this.

Attach to no one, to no thing. When you attach you are   6
looking elsewhere for your support. I AM the One you must
seek and need. When you seek Me I AM. I clothe the body. I
restore the form. I govern well. I radiate form intended. Be
with Me.

Let the Christ emanation in your heart be as the 7
light around you. Cast a glow. As you love, you express that
light *of the Christ appearance*. You love them as I love you.
This is the soul government on earth. Blessed are they
who find this.

You vibrate eternal oneness by loving. AM I not that love? 8
Let your heart be glad. Let the nature of your true self emerge.
I AM love.

Come To
The House
Of God

In the Mind of God all things are radiant and beautiful. 9

I AM in your heart and your mind. I AM activity 10
of consciousness as the I AM, as the Christ, vibrant
and free. I govern well. It is My system you seek. Come
to the house of God. It is the true government on
earth. When you operate from this system, good
government is returned and the lion lies down with
the lamb. I have government to offer you that is not of
this world.

As you allow Me to express as you, I act upon form *and* 11
form will change. I alter your form to conform to My plan of
excellence. Have your form in Me. I have come to dress you
in the mantle of light.

You are registered in My Mind as a child of light. I know 12
no other child in Me. Thus I call upon you to look to your
apparel *as light*. To reveal God is to reveal the Light of
the world.

As I, you never die. Have I not called you from the depths 13
of the grave? Where then is your faith?

Immortals never die, do they? Look to your immortal Self, 14
the I AM. Look not to your fleshly appearance. I unlock many
doors. I will unlock this one: I want My Spirit dominant on
the flesh. Look to the true Self and walk with Me. I AM
positive regrouping of forces.

Raise up your body in Me. And walk My plan. In Me there 15
is no death.

Be Clothed   My Consciousness becomes your consciousness in degrees 16
By Spirit   of understanding. As more and more of My Consciousness is
accepted and reigns supreme as your consciousness, so does
the fruitage begin to appear. I bear My own fruit. If there is
no fruit, there is no Creator.

✧ Think on the sacred Center of your being.   17

✧ Learn to express from that Center. In humility walk.   18

✧ Every word must come from the divine Center of   19
your Christ life. Every movement. Your divine center
is your Being.

✧ Learn to express from that divine Center. Have your   20
consciousness in Me.

✧ Be clothed with Me that I might always be with you   21
as pulsating life energy. I will reveal Myself, My Son's
life in you, through every atom of your being. This is
the ascension message, the resurrection and the life,
the new code of life distributed through every cell
and molecule by order of the Son of God!

✧ Wear your clothes well for I AM the cloth of your   22
being. I AM joy. I AM life. Clothe yourself with the
light that is your divine heritage. Anchor in the light
of My immortality in you.

✧ When you have found Me, you have found yourself.   23
You wear the immortal cloth of Be-ing. Your
consciousness and My Consciousness are One.
And the life force becomes your force. You are
immortal soul.

The   Beware of the mirror, the false claim on your life. Seek the 24
Omni-   holy Presence within you. *I AM your mirror.* When you seek
present   Me you will discover a new image. Forget for the moment
One   what you look like and remember Me. Then all humanity can
profit by your "good looks."

Gather not dust nor wrinkles of age. You are not old. You 25
have no age in Me. Be conscious of the mirror only as a
reflection of My Spirit. See the divine idea. Then others will
see it.

Attach to the reality, not to the false appearance. Let the 26
mark of My Spirit be on your face and throughout your whole
body. Accept the living light through your body and decree
you are one with It. Decree this frequently. I AM you. Let
your acceptance go very deep into the soul, the subconscious
mind. Let Me enter you. It is My Divine Idea I give you, not
the false cosmetics of man!

Your Christ at-one-ment brings new vital life power. 27
Subsequently you feel better, you look wonderful. You are
free of false ideas and illusion. I want you back as Myself!
Consciously. *I want you to know that you are with Me.*

You are vital, free and in My Spirit. Leave the old 28
age concepts behind you. In My Spirit there is no age,
only the consciousness of divine godhood. You have no age
at all. Leave the mortal. Be one with Me. Together we are
immortal. Reverse the process of death and decay by
turning to our oneness of Being. I want every breath
you take to be of Me. Breathe the Breath of divine
life now!

Living in the Presence releases a balance that will enliven 29
your physical, mental and emotional expression. Reflected
through your body will be a joy of harmony: all cells working
together for good. The less you worry or concern yourself
with your body, its appearance, its health, and receive My
word only as divine intelligence in you, the greater breadth
you will have as the body of light.

Count your blessings, then decree them. The divine Center 30
is your body. Take on the radiant appearance of My Heart's
Blood in you. You are My design. You are of Me. Let the
worldly appearance go. My Spirit harvests.

I Have A New Form For You

And I AM conscious of this new form in Me. I carry it. My 31 rhythm carries it. I embody it now.

Live the illusion no more. Look to the light. I AM the 32 Creator in you calling to be heard. Hear Me! Outer trinkets have no value. I have jewels for you greater than any you could buy. Let Me adorn you with new life and bless you with the jewels of perfection, the vibrations of My glory.

I have called you to respond to Me. Every activity of your 33 being must respond. Do not burden yourself with your appearance. Your outer appearance is of no concern to Me. Take upon yourself a new appearance. Let the mortal shell drop away. *I give you life.* Then beauty will shine through you as radiance of the soul.

When the Voice of My Consciousness takes root in you, it 34 is the glory of My Being. It is the station of Myself. It is My government. You shall have this Voice. You shall walk in My will, ever conscious of My supreme intelligence in you. And then shall you know Me as I AM, the God in you.

Letting Go Of The False Image

As you seek and accept the true appearance for My life's 35 sake, your body is translated into My rhythm and it becomes physically beautiful to behold. My breath becomes your breath. Bathed in light, you become lighter and lighter. The false personality or mask will drop away as you abide in Me. I AM all there is. In this truth stand, and have your being in Me.

The animal nature fades away, giving place in your awareness 36 to the Christ. You become the light of the world and the Mother breathes new life into you: it is the "I AM." Thus the word of Power is impressed. The God power in you is the I AM. How powerful is the creative word as it is spoken and decreed!

As you let go of the old and detach from the appearance, 37 the vital energy of the higher self emerges, causing great light in you and new strength to flow through you. You become afire with love. Such is the Supreme Being Who rises in your awareness to be. Your consciousness becomes My Consciousness. Such a union brings great happiness to the soul.

God rests His body in your heart that He might come to 38 Be. This is the Word made manifest. In such a way are you born anew into light and love. You cannot help but love yourself when you know who you are.

Thoughts of Power

1) Your body takes on new Thought; the radiation of the Supreme covers and enlightens you.

2) Personality fades as you have known it.

3) You are bathed in the light.

4) You are truly anointed in love, which is the Personality of the Christ.

5) The personal self, or sense of self, rises into the Impersonal Self. The life energy gives to the One. All becomes light. Intelligence reigns.

6) And here, in this place, you are welcomed as the prodigal son who has returned home.[1] No more do you search for home, for you have found it. You are one with God in you as I AM.

7) The fire is lit. You are fulfilled and this fulfillment gives you peace.

---

[1] See Luke 15:11-32.

CHAPTER TWENTY-ONE

You Are Love

You are seeing love, the absolute rhythm of God, around you 1
because you are love.

L et love flourish in you. Be rich in love. Every activity 2
should be love-filled. *Then you will be fulfilled.*

In your home, cook and clean in love. *Be in that rhythm.* 3
Feel it all about you. Feast on it. In your workplace be thankful,
and carry your gratitude in your heart to bless all whom you
meet. This thankfulness creates abundant supply in your life.
A thankful heart must be filled. It is the law.

✧ Take a moment to be thankful now and radiate out 4
to all this gratitude.

✧ The God-awakened individual is always thankful. 5

✧ Let your love flow and embody. It will objectify in all 6
your life. You cannot help but be surrounded by love
if you give it.

**Your
Attitude**
You are what you think and feel. You embody the Creator 7
in motion. Therefore, love beyond endurance, for you are
love. Love puts God in motion.

I have all the love you need. I AM the outpouring of My 8
Son's life in you. There is no division. Draw on Me for I
come as the Creator in you. I will baptize you in My love.

**Let My
Records
Live**
Judge not one another for I AM all in all. My creation is 9
perfect—without disorder, chaos of any kind. I create no
disorder in Me. Become *Christ* conscious. Dwell not on the

unreal. The final days are here. I unlock the records of Man's life and say, I AM after the Order of Melchizedek.

Human death is no more. Forget what has gone before. 10 Let the records live of My Son's life in you, the supreme son of all creation. When you seek Me I come and release you of all that is of the lower dimension.

Everyone you meet is a sister, a brother. This has absolutely 11 nothing to do with church membership nor blood family. Brotherhood and sisterhood are your recognition of Truth: the rhythm of My being weaving Itself through all life.

In the Presence of God there is no separation and no one is 12 left behind. That is the message of Christ through *all* civilizations.

Wherever you stand in the recognition of My reality, that 13 place is "holy ground." It is the place of My abundant nature. It is a vortex of My Creative Power and love. I AM there. Qualify Me by your recognition. Honor Me. Nowhere can you go where I AM not. This now becomes a mandate of My creation.

Come Dance With Me

Love, indeed, surrounds you. The caring love of the Creator. 14 Dance in this love. Be in it. See the reality through the flesh. *Become alive in Me.* Dance with the masters of all creation. Dance with the angels. Come live in Me in My creation and be joyful.

How My heart bursts with the desire to be! Glory upon 15 glory, life upon life. My Spirit embodies love. As joy fills your being, it is I. You are born of My joy.

CHAPTER TWENTY-TWO

True Vision

You cannot see with mortal eyes. No sight is there. 1
Once you stabilize in the real, that which is not dissolves;
for it has no reality in Me.

N ow the troubled world disappears and a new world of 2
light begins to have power in your life. See this world as
My foundation and build on that.

Reestablish yourself in the creative power I AM and allow 3
that power to express as your vibratory axis. As you do
this, you lock into the holy spheres of love and light, the
Christ Sphere.

Keep The Mother In Your Heart The Mother as your creative power translates all life into 4
qualified rhythms, energies of My Being. And lo, I AM pleased.
Such a day now beckons as I return the Mother to the throne
of your awareness. The vibratory record must include the
Mother. In Her you find your life and your creative power. It
is in the Mother, the womb of God, that all things are born
to Be. I AM in expression is Be-ing.

Conscious of My creative power, you do not linger in the 5
mortal realm. When you know who you are, you respond. So
that you know, these records are released and given unto you.
That you will remember. The Consciousness of Christ is your
membrane of divine intelligence. It enables you to know the
truth and to be it.

I seek to establish My Kingdom on earth as the living Truth. 6
From the Mother Office this whole light will be given. All
things born of Her will come to pass.

I hold a mirror up to you that you might see Me. I stand as 7 peace in you. If you would but come to Me you would know peace.

I AM the Word peace. Have this peace. As you learn to 8 listen to My Christ Voice in you, you will raise this Earth to her new consciousness which is the Land of Milk and Honey.

I will draw all My lights together into a Mighty Son, a true 9 and triumphant Sun! Together, as the mighty I AM Presence, you will bring peace as *consciousness* to Earth. My government is love. *I have unlocked the records for you that you might know the Truth.*

I AM with you but I must be with you in all your life 10 expression. Rise now out of conformity into the originality of God's Spirit in you. Look not here nor there. Be lifted that you might see Truth. And in Truth form the new life. I give you peace. Yea, I give you life intended. Come.

CHAPTER TWENTY-THREE

Give Me Your Heart

God's sanctuary is in your heart. I AM there.   1
Remember to look to that place for your sanctuary.

For there in your heart is the place of God   2
where love abides.

The love that so many seek and often cannot find   3
is there—at rest—in the heart.

There in that place where you find the Christ, the living 4
Heart of God, is the place of stabilized being, the place
of *Christ Consciousness*, the place of life itself. Go there in
your need, in your hunger to be recognized and loved. It is
there, in the wholeness of your being, you will be fulfilled
and recreated in mind and spirit. It, the heart, is the holy
sanctuary of My Son. In that placement I and the Father are
one unified being. In this place all things are recreated and
requalified.

Therefore, when you cry out, "Nobody loves me!" or hear 5
that cry from another, loose and go free in Me. Release that
consciousness that is alone and forsaken. Come home. The
home is the sanctuary of the Heart. In that way you are loved.

Release the appearance—whether it is "good" or "bad"— 6
it matters not. Let go. And enter into the selfless position of
Christ which is the Heart. Rise and be qualified, yea *recognized*,
as the loving and glorified Son-Daughter of God. Behold
I AM!

Remove all doubts from your system. Let go! Dive into 7
the waters of My Spirit. Feel the Life Force about you as My

waters cover you with My Will. I will guide and direct you and abide with you.

As you dive into the waters of God, take nothing with you 8 other than your love of God, your desire to give to God all that is you: your life, your family, your possessions. Give back to God that which is His. And forget the past. There is new order in the Kingdom. An order of Creative Power and everlasting Life.

Here is the secret: Just Be. Without expectations for a good 9 life or a bad life. *Be.* This is the way of the Spirit. Therefore, let go of your ideas of what constitutes a "pleasant" life or a "comfortable" life. As you truly enter the "eye of the needle," take nothing with you but your own deep desire to be in My world as one with Me. As you can do this and not judge your world, so more and more God will be on the field as Be-ing. And this divine life is you.

Now go into the sanctuary of the Heart. And there release 10 the flesh—all that has been a part of your life so far. Release into Me that I might live. And so shall you come home—as the fabled phoenix—"Another and the same."

CHAPTER TWENTY-FOUR

Universal Selfhood

You are worthy. 1
You carry My Son's Life in you.

Have I not made you 2
in My image and likeness?

The totality of *Being* is your Christ Consciousness. Once 3
the Christ is born in you *as* you, It, like a young child,
will command all of your attention. Therefore you must
nourish It, put Its welfare above who you think you are. This
is the Mother Principle coming to the fore once again.

In the Christ the whole is always considered. Thoughts go 4
to the whole, not the part. Thus selfishness must go; self-
greed of all sorts and kinds. The universal rhythm of the Christ
must be maintained and *exercised*. The Babe must be rocked
by the Mother in the supreme position of the "I AM." Such
a motion will shut out darkness and call forth the creative
power of the Divine One.

Here is a suggestion for you: If and when your thoughts 5
drift to the limited sense of self, turn those thoughts again to
the indwelling God Presence, the Christ, and harvest that
Consciousness. Train those spiritual thought and feeling
muscles! Activate them. Align them to the regions of light
where all things are possible.

In recent years there has been an emphasis on eating healthy 6
foods and exercising the physical body. Now I want you to
exercise the spiritual muscles. Just as your physical exercise
program has taken discipline and dedication, so now must

your spiritual exercise program demand of you equal time and dedication.

No one can run the mile for you. No one can drink the 7 carrot juice for you. No one can exercise your spiritual alignment muscles. Only you can do this. Therefore take your attention off the problem, the appearance, the "little self" and put your undivided attention on Christ within. That is the way to the Holy of Holies, the gateway to the Everlasting.

Being In Me

Let your Son rise in you, your own expression as "I AM." 8 Today I want you back with Me consciously. I want you to know that I AM with you in all ways. Ways that you have not conceived of yet. You are My transparency. We are one.

Come to the place I have provided. Here is the key to 9 existence. You must turn it. Enter. I will fill you with My completeness. Dwell not on the unreal. Come.

I AM the door. The door to your conscious awareness rests 10 in the Christ Center of your being. I AM you. I AM the oneness of all life in you as I AM. Honor Me and nourish Me, for I AM you. *Consciousness knows Itself as I AM.*

I AM conscious of you in Me as you return to be with Me. 11 I know then that you are part of Myself. We can do all things together. At one. Lift your thoughts to Me. There is the power. There is right action. Free yourself in Me.

In Me you find your strength. In Me you find your purity. 12 So it is that you cannot live without Me, nor I without you. We are one unit of perfection. When you know this, you are free. Have your being in Me. I AM the truth in your system. The Omnipresence. I build My house upon your belief. As you consciously accept the Christ in yourself and nourish this One, you will know that you are worthy to receive Me as the "I AM" of yourself. There will be no doubt in your mind.

A New Life

Value your true self. Know who you are. This value 13 judgment will affect your whole life. It will change your circumstances. Once you know who you are, you can meet all circumstances with Christ light. This is Omnipresent God in you.

Where I AM, you are. We are one. As you realize and become conscious of the Christ Consciousness you are, you are released from all past misconceptions. You cannot nor will you be attracted to the same circumstances and conditions that have been your experience. You begin a new life in Me. 14

When you continue to look to the Light of the God presence within your heart and nourish that Light, you become it in all ways. *The Law of Energy is: what you nourish is yours. You claim it by your focused attention to it.* If you will always focus your attention on the GodSelf, you become that One consciously. That is the plan of God for you. When this happens you are filled with My Life and the higher self rules. There is an overlay of Spirit that walks with you and gives you solace and peace. 15

When you nourish Me in you as I AM, the Christ Spirit or *Life,* you are undivided and have access to the Intelligence of God. The Christ mysteries are opened. The seal is broken. You manifest a degree of My Being on the Breath and you walk in the creative power: My Power of Love and Light. You are truly a radiation of God, a vibrant, creative, universal being. This is My plan for you in Me. 16

The GodSelf This universal field of Intelligence that I AM is ever conscious of Itself as you. It breathes intelligent life into you and is in all ways conscious of you *as Itself.* The electrodes know Me as I AM. There is no other life. I AM with you and there is oneness. In Me all things are made and unmade. 17

In the GodSelf, who you are, is all harmony and perfect order of Being. Here in this vibrant creative Be-ing is life as it is intended. It is the glory of God manifest. No longer can you wonder, "Am I worthy?" You live and have your life in 18

Me. And in this unity we have together, no thought of unworthiness comes. Raise your thoughts to Me.

One Mind   The Intelligence of God is your intelligence. As you draw   19
from that field of experience and are initiated into the I AM THAT I AM, the Divinity Circuit where I embody consciously, My Universal Life becomes who you are. You are recreated into My field of experience as the universal self. Therefore praise, adore and be centered in your GodSelf, for I AM that Self of you.

Have Your   Place your confidence in Me. I will not fail you. I unfold   20
Confidence   from within yourself. I complete you; I will express you and
In Me   reveal Myself through you as I AM. I AM the unbroken cord of life.

In Me you have your strength and power. Let   21
your confidence be in Me. Be centered and emptied so that I, the Christ within, might be in expression as your life. Any lack of confidence you might feel is corrected as you permit Me to express through you as the "I" of yourself. I do everything perfectly. God in you is perfect. Understanding this gives you greater confidence, does it not?

Depend on your Source. Your creative power will rise as I   22
decree. Then comes the manifestation in perfection of My Be-ing on the Breath. I that AM your source will radiate through your body, your mind, your soul as your supply. Your dependency on God within is imperative to strengthen you in your alignment to the Christ power.

Walk in faith. If the faith is there, all things are possible.   23
Faith is the cutting board, the creator of all life.

Walk   Be not of this world. Your world is not My world. Come   24
Faithfully   home. *Let the dead bury their dead.* (Matthew 8:22) You come
In Me   to Me that My world might express. Come into the place

that I have prepared for you and give yourself to Me. I AM That which is divine in you as the "I AM."

As you seek God, God is. I come and I AM. No mountains 25 to climb, nor initiations to pass. There are no steps in Me. The "fall of man" never happened in Me. I know it not. As you enter Me the "fall of man" does not exist. All illusion vanishes. *I have never fallen.* Stabilized in Me you know this.

One Conscious- ness

Jesus reclaimed you in Me as he walked this planet Earth. 26 He returned you to Me consciously, and he gave birth to a radiant new idea of your Christ identity. He bequeathed you to Me in a radiant new form of being, the Son of God Himself. Know this, for in Christ you are formed anew. He transferred you into Me by his Incarnation.

When you "accept Jesus into your heart," you realign your 27 consciousness to his and you become a part of his transformation. You are a part of his record. As you receive him, you are restored and regenerated. The Master Jesus accepted you first within himself, and as a human wearing the same flesh as you, he gave you to Me *as a living part of himself.* Now he stands with you *as I AM.* Please study this last statement. Contemplate it. It will have meaning for you. In the nature of his transference, you are made anew in him. This, then, becomes the cornerstone for a new humanity: a deathless humanity raised in light.

The Creator, who saw Himself through Jesus, breathed 28 new life into your form. As the one you know as Jesus wore the fleshly robes of the human being, so he became *you* for an instant. In that moment of time, Jesus was able to transform earth creation. He canceled out the lie and he rose *as you* in Me. Would you but know this you would be free.

Delivered Of All Shame

Yet, all that I know is My Son's life in you. For Me that is all 29 *there is.* There is no other. How can you deny that Universal Self within you that is the Christ? Heed that Light, that living and conscious Seed within your heart. Nourish It. It is the embodiment of all I AM. Arise in Me!

Many are bound in shame right now. They are unable to 30 accept Me, bound as they are by the turmoil within them. These ones are bound by the lies of the world. They are bound by false appearances. If these ones were to receive Jesus and his path, they would discover the plane of union where *I and the Father are one*. They would be with Me in him. Can you not see this?

Jesus said, *Behold! I AM the resurrection and the life.* (John 31 11:25) Whoever will thirst for righteousness will be satisfied. And whoever hungers after Me shall be fed. My river never runs dry. I AM the beginning and the end. And when there is darkness, I AM the light. Have you lost sight of who you are? I came that you might see *and My presence remains.*

Enter Me   The goal of every human being is to become one with God. 32 This may be a hidden goal. But it is there.

The joy of My Spirit permeates all cells and gives new life. 33 Deny not what is within you. As you learn to live in the Christ now, delivered of all shame, you create out of yourself a world of light, a heaven on earth.

I AM the Omnipresent Christ in you. Let go of the past, 34 for I AM not there. That is yesterday's manna! I AM here with you now, in this moment as the Presence of God. Let Me live in you. I AM now.

Live by My Breath alone. Live by My Light. For I have 35 come through you to light the way for others.

I AM the resurrection and the promise. Therefore be not 36 overcome by the world. I ask you, do not believe in it. *Believe in Me.* Farther are My horizons than you can see. I will show you by My Spirit. I will cover you with the fire of My life.

Let My Presence cover you, My Spirit dwell within. I have a 37 nesting place *within you.* I AM the Christ Seed placed in your heart. Come to Me. Seek Me first. Whatever your desire may be, whatever your need, let Me embody. I AM THAT I AM.

I AM the answer to your every question. I will be with you 38
as you seek Me before all else. In My divine substance you are
replenished, made whole again in Me. I AM abundant, joy-
filled life threaded through all My creation. Seek first
the Kingdom.

Always seek Me as your highest good. Learn to trust in 39
Me. Develop that trust. Practice it. Build your faith. Then
can I give you *out of Myself* all things you need. I AM abundant
life in expression now. Why don't you come Home where I
AM? Let Me love My creation through you.

**Learn
The True
Seasons
Of The
Self**   Know that nothing is lost in Me. Downward slides may 40
come, you may feel depressed, or without motivation.
However, learn to use these times appropriately. Do not let
them use you! When a rest is indicated, take it. Slow down
when indicated. Creation takes place in the dark womb of the
soul, within the Divine Mother Herself *where I AM*. Waiting
is a lesson learned, patience a gift of the Spirit. Have the
patience to wait on Me.

Wait for My motivation in you. I spark you as the living 41
light. Your highest goals will be achieved as I rise in you. Let
Me unfold.

❖ There are seasons to My Life.   42

❖ When incubation is indicated, be at peace.   43

❖ Let My Spirit bring forth the new.   44

❖ Empty and be still.   45

❖ It is often in the times of stillness, when nothing seems 46
to be happening, that I birth in you My life.

❖ Have the confidence and the patience to move and 47
have your being in the seasons of My Be-ing.

❖ Let go and let God.   48

❖ Rest in the divinity of your person and trust in That. 49

❖ I AM not anxious. Neither should you be.   50

❖ Are we not one?   51

CHAPTER TWENTY-FIVE

Take No Bows

Let My rhythm be your rhythm.   1
Practice the God Center.
It will answer you with life.

Take no bows. As you come to Me there is no need for 2
things of the world. Resist the need for accolades. Do
not seek to please man "whose breath is in his nostrils." (Isaiah
2:22) I have far better things for you than man's praise.

Bold is My resurrection in you. Creative is My expression. 3
God sends His light through you to express God. I AM the
resurrection and the life! If you but seek Me, *I AM*. Come,
be with Me. Let My Consciousness be your consciousness. I
glorify the Christ in you.

I AM intelligent energy through you. *Life itself.* When the 4
ego (sense of self) seeks acclaim, return to Me, your
omnipresent Self. With the Apostle Paul, declare: *I am
crucified with Christ: nevertheless I live; yet not I, but Christ
liveth in me.* (Galatians 2:20)

Praise and be thankful to the Life circuit you are. 5
Be not prideful at any time. Seek no power for yourself.
God is the only power. Say that. Seek the unified field of
original creation and be there with Me. Then, recircuited,
say "I AM."

I AM the rock upon which you must stand. The tune 6
you must play. My children want peace yet they seek Me not.
Come to the place where there *is* peace. Come to Me. When
you have Me, you have all life in balance. I AM the perfect
Adjuster. Come Home to Me so that I might rise in you as
I AM.

Letting Me   I AM selfless service. Let Me serve in you as My Word and 7
come forth as your Be-ing. Come to Me and let Me rise into
direct expression. I AM desirous *to be*. I wish to live and have
My Presence known.

When you seek first the Kingdom of God and His right- 8
use-ness, you allow Me to express directly. I embody My Son's
Life in you. My will becomes your will. I translate your body
then. You enter My Kingdom or Consciousness where all that
I have is yours.

Can you not see, dear one, when you give yourself to Me 9
in love, you allow Me to vibrate through you as your true
Self? This is the program of My life circuit. I want you God
conscious.

Remember that you must be willing to lose your life to 10
find it. As you give yourself to Me, you are permitting Me to
be. And in Me you have life and have it abundantly. Behold,
I shall make all things new!

Be Christ   Seek no man's applause. When you look to another for 11
Centered   rewards, you lose your connection with Me. *I AM the One
you seek*. Listen to the words I speak, for they are true.

I AM the way, the truth and the life. Seek to please Me. 12
When you seek to please Me only, I will translate you. You
will ascend with Me. I will carry you further than light itself.

Here is the key: Give Me what you receive. For   13
it is in My Hands that all things turn to good.

Remember, O My suns of God, My spiritual power leaves 14
when you seek the praise of man. Serve not man but God. Be
God centered.

Recall the words of Jesus, the wayshower, when he said: "I 15
of my own self can do nothing." My Son Jesus recognized
Me as the power in his life. I would that you would do the
same. He called Me forth with his recognition. Thus we

formed a oneness, a unified field of intelligence. My breath became his breath, My light, his light. We were one. You are best served to follow his example. Here is the perfect balance of the equation. Your formula for life everlasting.

I Wear The Title Well

Let spiritual ambition be gone. Take your mind off "self" 16 and put it on Me. In Me all things are made. *For I AM the substance of all life.* In Me you will find peace without the mask of personality.

Many are caught in phenomena, often attaching themselves 17 to various names and titles. As you receive any kind of recognition, *return it to God.* This is the testing ground. *Everything goes back to the One.*

Open your heart that I might be. Be empty that I can fill 18 you. Let not false tributes fill your head nor mortal accolades estrange you from Me. AM I not the glory you seek? Call yourself minister? Call yourself priest or priestess? Always remember to receive Me in you *as who you are.* Be ever watchful of spiritual pride. I have no place for that in Me. Think upon this and know My place in you. Be quickened and ever mindful we are one. In our unity we are a shining Sun!

Consciousness beholds Itself as One. Are you ready to stand 19 in this embodiment? Then stand in this conscious awareness, meeting it in your daily life. In Truth, there is one Consciousness: the Allness proclaiming Itself as you.

Take My Harvest

When you subject yourself to the inner power of My divine 20 radiance, you find others are drawn to you. Some might say you have "charisma." It is the marriage of light with man. All those who come to you are drawn by the energy of the Christ, the holy Sun of yourself. I send them to you that I may teach them through you. I AM drawn to them and they are drawn to Me. We are united in your love and by your light.

The more you nourish and contemplate your Christ Self, 21 the GodSelf, the greater is your capacity to love. You have come to share My love with all My creation, *every one.* You have come to give them My portion.

Have the harvest of My perfection. As you expand in Christ 22 revelation (who I AM in you), you will be called upon to serve as never before in the light of My Being. Great will be your work in Me!

Fear not, nor be apprehensive of seemingly powerful people, 23 for there are no "powerful people" in Me. Positive alignment with the Creator moves mountains. There will be storms, but they will not touch you. Tend My flock. They are brought to you by Me. Stand ready to give to them what I give to you.

Better that you do not follow the leading of others but, 24 instead, listen to the GodSelf. Be centered and value your true being, the one who you are.

Lean not on others. As you look to another, the Word will 25 weaken and lose its life in you. The Word is My Consciousness in you. When you dwell in Me and allow Me to dwell in you, My energy will fill you. You will feel My light in you and know My truth.

Yea, you shall be covered with My Breath and be deepened 26 in My Spirit. I will breathe in you and you will be full-filled.

CHAPTER TWENTY-SIX

Have the Courage to Be

Allow now the Christ within you 1
to do the work.

He that is within is your GodSelf. 2
And He who will not leave you
is your Truth.

The conception of the GodSelf is the transfiguration of 3
your consciousness. You have a *responsibility* to see the
Truth. You have learned how important it is to nourish your
God Center, the place wherein the Child of Light dwells. I
AM your indwelling Creator, the Child whispers. Even as
Mary, the mother of Jesus, nurtured this wondrous Child, so
must you. This Child *is you*. It is your true identity, the
omnipresent Consciousness of God in you.

Continue to nourish the Christ Seed within your heart. 4
When you do this, your spiritual nature lives in grace and
freedom, and this God presence will reflect outwardly as your
experience and your life. This is why the Master Jesus advised:
But seek ye first the kingdom of God, and his righteousness; and
all these things shall be added unto you. (Matthew 6:33) Yet it
is important to remember that you must also nourish the
Christ Self within every human being. This is what
unconditional love is. It is the presence of this awareness.
When you love in this way, all life fuses in your consciousness
as the One. You see anew. This "One" is the unified field of
potentiality and your God potential.

See With New Eyes

Honor the GodSelf within all life. Honor Me. Then as you 5 walk in harmony with nature, you will feel My presence everywhere. Really see the presence of God in all life. See Me there. I created unbroken life that I might be. Let the suffering go.

If you criticize and see evil in others, you will take that 6 which you "see" upon yourself. As you allow God to be in you, then God will vibrate as your life. Seek first the Kingdom of God. In this way are you filled and entered into My Book of Life. What you see in another is often within you. Seek Me in your neighbor and I will show you the greater part.

In the words attributed to the Apostle Paul: *For now we see* 7 *through a glass, darkly; but then face to face: now I know in part; but then shall I know even as also I am known.* (I Corinthians 13:12) As the Christ emerges through your mind and your heart, your vision is repaired. Blessed are they who see clearly in this day. To see clearly *is to know.* Never lose sight of that.

Keep Your Eye Single

Make no comparisons. Remember I AM. Forget the past 8 and let your GodSelf shine! Many leave the past only to return to it. I AM not the past. I AM now. In this way do you translate into God Be-ing.

Be conscious of Me in you. Give yourself to Me that I 9 might be. In this way do you receive My word and My God radiation. *I AM with you in your acceptance.*

Be subject to inner laws, the laws of My Being. As you 10 follow your own path, not the path of another, your divine personality will emerge: a vibrant new self. I will dress you in fine clothing.

I have brought you into this place to know Me. I AM one 11 with your heart-center. I AM the Light of the world! Listen to the Christ within. Behold, He is with you. And lovingly take this Christ as your Self.

My Body Is Light

Rely on the Christ within. You are translating out of an old 12 body into a new. The more you rely on the Christ within, the more the Christ will radiate through you *as living light.* This Christ Consciousness becomes your consciousness. The reliance on the Christ Center (God within) turns the key and the door will open to a new day.

You are a creative being. You are blessed by My Being in 13 you as I AM. If you will turn to your Christ Center you will create a motion of consciousness that vibrates unity with God. This is My promise. As you learn to live in My Presence, you become that Presence. You activate It. You become the life I AM.

I AM with you always. Your needs are My needs. Thus 14 every decree is of My Holy Voice. *My Spirit.* You release creative power when you speak. And all things are given as I have promised. I translate you out of the world.

As you seek to please Me, I shower you with My blessings. 15 Can you not see that when you bend and bow to another, when you seek approval from friends and relatives, when you desire praise and love from those around you, that you have separated yourself from Me? He that comes to Me is always fulfilled.

Look to Me and you will be comforted. My Spirit is with 16 you and proclaims Itself as unconditional love. He who comes to Me is fulfilled and he is supplied.

My Word Is Government On Earth

My fountain never runs dry. AM I not the Creator of all? 17 Listen to My Spirit within. Heed My call. Walk in My Way, the way of the Creator in you as I AM.

With what majesty you will walk then! With what dignity! 18 Walk in the way of My Son Jesus who is original creation in you as blueprint for humanity. He was sent *as the way.* He is the path. His are the footprints on the sand. Come follow me, he said. So do so now. Follow him.

As I speak, you will know Me. You will always know 19
that it is I. *My sheep know My Voice.* You have the ability
to discern. My Inner Voice is always confirmed by the
presence of the Holy Spirit. We are never separate. You will
know My words are true, for the Christ presence dwells
within the sound and the whispered breath. We are both
beautifully entwined as the Voice of guidance and direction
in your life. You have but to seek us and we are there, the
Father and the Son who bless you with the presence of
Holy Spirit.

My Son lives with Me in a testimony of grace. I have 20
resurrected him to be with you as My Voice. When I decree,
I do so in his alignment or name. This arranges the molecules
of your universe in proper sequence.

Therefore seek the Son in you and return to the beginning, 21
the place where I AM. I AM the Light of the world in you as
I. And that which is given unto the Son (Jesus' embodiment
on earth), is given unto you also through him as divine
blueprint.

As the power is given, it goes through him as Christ to 22
you. As the light is given, so it is given through him to you. I
have established a great temple upon this earth. *I have called
it Sananda.*[1]

**The Word
Is Law**
Consciousness is law. When Jesus walked this earth he 23
created a new humanity out of himself. Now you are feeling
the result of his ascension. It is the time for all to rise and
ascend to love and light. Be awakened!

I stand with Him in you as I AM. This is why I ask you 24
not to "channel." I would urge you to find the God Center
within your heart and in this place know I AM.
We are one in this place.

I have established the Garden of Eden within you. I AM 25
the living channel of your grace.

---

[1] Sananda is the ascended name of Jesus. It—the name—remains as a lifting presence on
our planet.

Did not My Son say, "I and my Father are one"? (John 26
10:30) Therefore that is the declaration of Law on this planet
and cannot be otherwise. See that you understand this clearly.

As Jesus stands with Me you will feel his presence and know 27
that it is the presence of the living Christ released on planet
Earth. This is My testimony to you. I say again: My Son and
I are One. No one can change that. No one can alter My
Word. He who is called is My Word spoken of Me from the
beginning as the living Message of "I AM." God speaks to
you through the Melchizedek order of My Son's Universe.

Give Me   I AM the Life in you that was decreed from the beginning. 28
Voice   When you seek Me, you will find Me. *Have no other gods
before Me. (Exodus 20:3) I AM the One sent. Do not listen
to "voices" but seek the one Voice that vibrates as the Son,
the Living Christ in you. Then shall you know and walk
unfettered.

Listening to My Voice brings you peace. My Spirit attends 29
you. And I know you as My Son of Light.

In Sonship we are one mind. There is no other. I AM with 30
you and you are with Me. There is no separation. We are one
Consciousness and that Consciousness is rightly named "I
AM." As you make this transition into the superconscious
mind, the mind of God, so do the angels hear you and obey,
for you think the thoughts of Me. There is no compromise in
you; we walk together now as one vibration as the GodSelf, a
living universe. A covering of My Holy Spirit over and around
you protects you from all harm. *You are Sun of God after the
Order of Melchizedek.*

Therefore, rise to this place that I have provided and be 31
with Me now. Let your consciousness rest in My
Consciousness. We are One.

Watch that you do not look to another for guidance 32
or love, but enter My sanctuary and call upon Me, and I

shall answer. Many come with their promises but I come as eternal life.

No Other Master   The GodSelf is the Master, no other. Therefore, 33 enlightenment comes from your beingness in Me. I tell you to seek first the Kingdom within and all else will follow. This is the ordination of the Supreme. He who comes to this is transfigured in My name. Seek Me in you and all else will follow. Glory forms of itself. Worship no one save the inner light.

Your "master" is the Inner Life. Always that is so. It is 34 from this degree of consciousness that the Master will appear. Christ within will unfold as the Voice, the beautiful, wondrous, rich new testament of life. When you know yourself in truth, you will have found your master.

The designated master may appear in human form, yet 35 he/she will always be that divine center of yourself.

You conceive of this Teacher. You give "Him" or "Her" 36 life. As you consciously align with the divine oneness, the Christ within, the Teacher will appear. You allow that one to appear and be with you in the Christ presence. It is up to you. It is your job to align.

The day of deliverance is near. There is no other Teacher 37 but the personification of the "I AM" Presence within your heart.

There Is No Master In Truth, Only I AM   As you keep your eye single and agree with that Light within 38 your heart and soul, so will the Word follow and bless you with Its divine presence. That is why it is said, "The master will appear when the student is ready." For the readiness is your willingness to *be*. Such is the way of Truth and the key to your revelation.

The only master is consciousness divine. Remember that, 39 child. For great is My wisdom in you.

Good Points To Remember

1) Once centered in Christ as the Son/Sun, all nature is obedient to My Voice in you. *Because we are One.* Be still and receive My Being in you. My Breath is your breath and we are one.

2) There is no greater gift than the Christ Child, the divine idea within you. This is the divine gift of creation. When you know and have accepted this gift in your heart, you have all things. There is nothing I would not give My Son, Who is of Me as I AM.

3) You have but to thank God and God will be with you.

4) False masters are everywhere. I say, come to the place I have provided: It is the Christ within yourself. Once the Seed opens, the true master will be revealed. The Omnipresence is the only master in truth. Such is the path for the initiate.

5) As you come to Me by your own choice, you are then initiated into the GodSelf of the Creator. Such an initiation brings instant results. Your personality changes into creative intelligence. The Divine Breath of all creation only serves the Master, the GodSelf within. Such a Life have I in you. As we create together, the greatest fire in life is ignited. I AM you. After the Order of Melchizedek.

PART 3

The Mind and Heart

*Your heart is the passageway
into the higher mind,
or the superconscious mind.*

*If you have love unconditionally
for all life,
you will transmute the lower
base energies
into Creator Thought.*

*Enter now
the intelligent realm
of Being.*

CHAPTER TWENTY-SEVEN

Concepts and Reality

In the Mind of God or Mount Zion, the summit of all revelations, 1
reality is realized. It is to this mountain that you are called.
God Consciousness is your creative mind. All that you are in Me.

As you dive into the sea of realization the sacred waters 2
cover your head and enter your bloodstream. Sacred
waters become you.

Return Where I AM, you are. We are one universal Be-ing. 3
To The God Hold now to the Mind of Truth as creation stirs under a 4
Center program of universe light. There are sacred laws you must
learn once again. They are not unfamiliar. They are the laws
of oneness and Be-ing. *I am not accustomed to separating*
Myself. I know no separation in Me. I have set this "time" aside
for My own Being to know Myself.

In this period of the dismantling of old concepts and 5
patterns, yea even old flesh, the Mind of God is recreating
Itself *deliberately,* as the Master of all creation enters into the
Mind of Creative Power, there to bestow Himself upon all
races and peoples of the world. When this happens, and it will
happen, the new creation embodies as the personal vibration
of your Jesus-Son, life content of man and God at one. It is
with this *new material* that I will form My new universe. I
will behold Myself in you. This is the power of the new
creation. I have completed one circuit. Now you will enter
another. Then shall you know who I AM.

Voluntary entrance into this Mind of God centeredness is 6
occurring. As you find yourself entering this plane, so shall
you know I AM.

The sacred light of God fills your being. All sons rise into 7
My Son of Light! Come to the place I have provided in Me.
You are mortal no longer. Let go. Forget the past. Seek that
which is given and align with that. I have governed you unto
this place that you might govern Me.

My Kingdom Rest in the truth that there is only one Mind: that is the 8
Is At Hand Mind of God or Divine Mind. All else is illusion. Forget the
past. Even as you seek to find Me, I AM with you. We are not
apart although it may seem as though you have traveled in
matter. We are attached in the creative circuit of I AM.

Thus, as you stabilize in the Mind of God, your contact 9
with and realization of the one Mind cause vibratory
agreement. This, in turn, will release you from the "lie" and
cause creation, or actualization of the truth, in every avenue
of your experience. You leave one dimension for the next.

It is necessary to understand the order of Mind. Love will 10
transmute all negative thought and action. The situation
changes when you can love unconditionally without thought
of reward for yourself. (This is really what Jesus meant by
turning the other cheek.) Thus you water your garden of
identity and true being. You testify to the oneness of all life,
My order.

I AM Me in you as I AM. This is the creative order of My 11
circuit. My place of residence and divine Be-ing. AM I not you?

Decree When you learn to live in the Presence, nothing is 12
From Me impossible. Raise up your consciousness. Join My Son's Life
in you as I AM. This is the creative potential, the living decree
of My life. Once stabilized, you are one with it. It becomes in
you the sacred life energy waiting to be decreed. *I AM waiting
for you to say "I AM."*

Raise up your consciousness. Nothing is complicated in 13
reality. For the life is My own. So *be* it. Create from your own

inner being. Release Me in you as the I AM. This will bring the creative power into focus and join you with Me *consciously.*

Be guided by the Spirit within and anticipate the moments 14 of silence that we have together. *Silence is substance.* It is the firmament of unlimited potentiality.

With Me (I AM) you can do all things, accomplish miracles 15 and be released of all karmic debt. Here is the master key. We (God and man) must together be creators of light. The I AM is singular. It is the Presence within you as your creative power. It can only be released through oneness, the order of the Living Light.

We are joined in a loving relationship that is always One. 16 My heart meets your heart in the glorified frequency of Being. *I AM.* In this place we decree as One. Here you acknowledge the frequency of My power, the Omnipresence of My light. Come to this place and decree. Have Me in you as the power and the light. Creative power is yours as you accept it. I call you forth as one with Me to receive My Word as Consciousness and to release My Consciousness *as your own.*

The divine decree is I AM. These are My words to you as 17 you learn to listen to the current of Universal Mind and follow My direction in you.

Heed the words of the Master, for these are My last days. 18 These are My days of resurrection and realization. I release you into light, the light of My higher intelligence in you. Listen, for you will hear My Voice and know My thoughts. The divine decree is within you.

The Omni-present Power Of God

Times of acute emptiness—it will seem so, although you 19 will be swimming in creative impulse—are My creative periods in you. You will sense an emptiness *before I fill you.* Therefore, take the emptiness with good faith (even as My son Jesus taught you to have faith in the unseen).

Faith is the substance or My creative power,   20
by which the form is realized and actualized.
It is the current of My substance. In faith
you know, and I AM That which is known.
Faith is the omnipresence of God come alive
in you.

Bring your faith to what seems to be emptiness and I will 21
fill you. I AM the presence of all that you need. Be with Me.
I AM with you yet I cannot express until you make a place for
Me. I empty you to fill you with the richness of My Being.
Such is the way of My world. Let My Mind operate through
you, then you are sustained and stabilized in grace. Where
you are conscious of Me, I AM. I AM complete in Myself as
perfect expression.

I have a new testament for you. You have been called to a 22
new rhythm of Intelligence, that of the Order of Melchizedek.

Rest in the eternal light of your soul. I summon you 23
to a world of light. I AM the Christ within. If you walk
with Me, you will never die, nor will you ever go hungry.
I AM the radiation of pure Be-ing, the sunlight of the soul.
Come home.

Heed the presence of God in you and listen. Let go of old 24
crystallization, old ideas and thought forms that are not of
Me. You and I are one. We are one. Think with Me in the
light of God Consciousness.

In Me you find all that you need. I AM the power of God 25
within you. I AM the creative power that seeks to express and
embody. I AM all things in you that are needed and
recognized.

Take My existence as your existence and let Me be in you. 26
Together we are One. We have never been separated except
by human thought.

An Affirmation

Based in perfection, I always AM.   27
This means that I am one with God at all times.
I am one with the Presence of God.
I *know* I AM.
I emanate God's presence and think with God's mind.
I am never apart from God.
Since God is ever present as my reality,
My movements are one with God's movements.
I am in the universal rhythm I AM.
I do not question what I do nor how I think.
I know the presence of God is with Me.
Thus I can say I AM at peace
and divine love is flowing
through every cell of my body.
I am alive in joy.

Divide Me Not

My Presence is in all life. *It is the creative substance.* If you 28 are experiencing error, you are operating out of duality or illusion. Return home to Me, the center point of your nature. See Me in all life. When you are conscious of Me, all error vanishes. *It can be contained only in your consciousness. It has no life of its own.*

Error is without power of its own. Adjust your vibration 29 (out-picturing as your life) by correcting your viewpoint. Let go of disharmonious thought forms and realign in the Presence. There AM I. And there you are also. Are we not one?

Hear My Voice and listen to the triumphant river of your 30 higher self. This is the Presence of the Life within you. When you readjust your conscious alignment to My wavelength, you can hear and know the light vibrating through every cell. Your molecular construction changes under My supervision. I AM that. And the Presence of God permeates every cell.

With Trust And Confidence Be The Light

All activity begins and ends in Me. Where I AM there is no 31 other. Align with the God Presence within you. Rest your heart and mind in that Presence and be at peace. Higher Mind overshadows the creative power determining its direction, affirming the power in you and *decreeing it*. Each vibration of agreement gives you a thrill of radiant love and perfect harmony. In Me all things decreed come to pass.

I want you conscious now, placed in My Son's Holy Sphere. 32 Are you not the Son of God in Me?

Receive Me: your own divinity within yourself. Let go of 33 past history. I have reseeded you in Me. This is the day of harvest. The great creative power will lift all into My Being. I AM the next dimension you are seeking. I AM the radiant spirit of pure being. The animal nature passes as you learn to live in the Christ Flame. *Identify with that.*

Your Church Is Within You

I AM waves of Intelligence and I come as Truth activated 34 by your faith in Me. Faith binds us. It completes us. Because you have been faithful, I have come.

Attend the church, the temple, within yourself. *Find Me in* 35 *you.* Am I not the church you have been seeking? Then come unto Me. Moment to moment attend Me. Keep Me in your consciousness. Sing hymns unto My Being in you. Rejoice. I shall never leave you nor shall I forsake you. I AM you.

Establish now the "return of Jesus the Christ" *in your heart.* 36 There is the sacred Son of your being. All comes from that. For what I speak of is the First Seed of Creation. I AM within you as the heart of you, the very soul of you. It is My heart that you feel beating in your chest. Where I AM there is no other heart. Hear My heart beating in you.

Listen to My word and deny not My power. I have come 37 to build My church in you. My church is within you *as you.* It is a place of quiet, of meditation. Attend your inner church daily. Live now joyously and abundantly in My church. Live in My rhythm.

Acknowledge The Creative Potential   Each little task has meaning. When you have division in 38 the workplace (as you separate Me from your job), you separate yourself from Me. *Everything you say and do is important.* Bring your whole self to every task. In My rhythm be. Love your work. Let Me be with you in every task. You will never tire if you do this.

Once the Christ Seed is opened and I AM released as 39 expression of your conscious awareness, I embody Myself. Give Me the opportunity to embody.

See through any situation that is as a prison to you. *All 40 conscious thought is there to be broken.* Free yourself. Walk free in universal understanding. Always seek enlightenment. Be free and allow My Spirit to pass through you. *I AM the light.*

Watch that you do not linger in a past memory or hunger 41 for the past. This could cause a snarl in your vital body, confusing your life energy. Stay in the now. When you need help call upon Me and I will answer.

See through religious theories and dogmas. Fear not. I AM 42 with you. I shall take you through each concept into the next. I AM living light. *Thus shall you learn greater truth than you have ever dreamed.*

I AM Melchizedek.[1] Come to Me that consciousness can 43 break into a million pieces and reform as the GodSelf, the temple I AM. Be lifted. What a life it is when we go from star point to star point in love divine.

From The Center Point   Opinions do not matter. Theories do not matter. It is My 44 Voice that matters, My Voice in you. Raise up your consciousness to the place where I AM. Dedicated to that flow, be in that Life Center that the creative power might express.

Live from your own center point, the governing point of 45 your own nature. If you stand strong in this place you cannot be controlled. You are your own person and live in your own

---

[1] Jesus has been identified as the high priest of the Order of Melchizedek. (See Hebrews 5) The Order of Melchizedek is the pathway to ascension and revealed Godhood.

light. You are vibrating the essence of your God Center. You can come and go as Christed energy in My Spirit.

Come to the God Center of your own being. Know who 46 you are. Keep yourself centered and the creative power will rise to express. *It wants to express and embody itself.*

Let the focus be on the Christ within your heart center.   47

No one is controlled in the God presence, the I AM. You 48 maintain your own equilibrium there and your own identity.

Who you are is maintained from the God Center.   49

This is the Ultimate program of the Creator. This is your 50 energy plan.

All harmony begins from your center point of awareness 51 and flows out as God in expression. This is stabilized grace.

Hear Me In You

As you put aside all your concepts to listen to the Inner 52 Voice within you, you will hear Me in you as the I AM Presence. I speak with light. And when I speak with light, I AM the Creator. I AM higher Intelligence grounded in you as your Active Mind, the mind that is creative and God centered. In Me you have light and this light is the illumined consciousness.

Put aside your concepts and listen to My Voice. *It is* 53 *illumination.* It is spontaneous and free *now. Nothing is brought forward from the past nor decreed for the future. I AM now.* When I speak as your Inner Voice in you, that which is given is of the moment. It is alive and active right now. I AM the creative power poised to form of itself.

Know that if you are willing to lay down your life for Me, I 54 will pick it up. I will enter you and be your life. The creative power registers at this point.

Let Go Of Criticism

What you criticize is really part of yourself. Subliminally, 55 you are trying to throw off the unwanted character trait and so you criticize another for the fault you carry within yourself. The minute you can face that trait within yourself and say,

"You have no power over me. You are not part of the Christ life!" the shadow substance will melt away. And you will no longer criticize another.

Can you see why it is important to be honest with yourself 56 and respond to every act of criticism with a look at yourself? Be not critical but align with Me. I AM perfect life in all souls. Nourish that Christ realization.

Judge not those who have been unfair to you. Forgive and 57 let go. *You are not to judge but to be reconciled to Me as the only law unto your person and your affairs.*

Remember also that you disturb your energy expression 58 when you criticize yourself unjustly. Here AM I. In this position the Truth will glow through your soul. Be anchored in the light. The Master never criticized, he knew the Truth.

Forget not that *I AM you.* Receive Me in yourself. Let us 59 live together, you and I, as individualized form in expression. What a wonderful life we have together, you and I!

Welcome the Light into yourself. Receive It. Respect your 60 whole Self. Agree with divine love, remembering always to let this love flow freely through your body, its cells and organs. *You are in a state of grace now.* You operate out of the same energy field that was with Jesus. You are as one who is born of divine love and God's purity. Accept Me in you and through you as I AM. We are one, you and I. Body, mind and spirit, we are one.

The Body Your body wants to express love. Every center of your being 61
Attunement wants to express love. But in order for your body to express love you must feed it love: care for it as you would a child, by agreeing with your Spirit nature.

Every cell is divine. See the Spark of Creation in every cell. 62 *I have permeated every cell by the light of Jesus.* Because he ascended, you have ascended in truth. *That is the Melchizedek Record.* You have but to agree with it that every cell of your physical body may be freed into the creative power. It is time to resurrect yourself into light. This is My completeness in you as the I AM.

Allow My presence to express through your whole 63 body. Let your body become light, as the living truth of Melchizedek shines forth in joy and in abundance. We are one.

A Word About Healing

Physician heal yourself[2] is wise counsel indeed.   64

A disagreement is not dissolved by sending light to another. 65 When you send light as an activity of your own consciousness, it is often the case that negativity accompanies the light. The consciousness of the beholder has not been lifted into the Christ.

It is often the case that the individual who sends light is 66 attempting to overcome evil with good. The "physician" has not healed him/herself. He or she is not "seeing" correctly. The "physician" must see anew.

Light is the activity of the Christ dimension. Therefore 67 in prayer and in all healing ministry, the healing must first take place *within* the healer's consciousness. That is to say: Take the power or energy out of the fight between good and evil. It is necessary to rise above the lie or appearance of good and evil into the realization of oneness.

To send light mentally to someone can cause a disturbance 68 within the individual you wish to help. *Don't attempt to change anything other than your own conscious awareness.* When you find the truth within yourself, the divine light of God is in expression.

Be still and know that I AM God. You do not have to correct 69 what is already perfect. When you can let the God Presence into your awareness things begin to happen, resulting in what might seem to be a miracle, but what is, in truth, right placement of energy. Let the I AM presence express. Then healing occurs.

---

[2] See Luke 4:23.

Release Old Habits

An old habit is nothing more than a false claim. Nothing 70 more. Habits are like crutches. Are you a prisoner of habit patterns?

In divine love there are no habit patterns, only the One 71 expressing in the moment as I AM. Tied to no one, "I AM" is in constant motion, ever declaring Itself and being Itself as declaration of Godhood and creative intent.

Be open and be flexible in the Holy Spirit I AM. As you 72 allow Me to express, old habits pass away. In Me is new life. You have only to let go of old habits and they are released from you; by your consent will they pass from you. Give up what you do not need. Release and be. For you are being escorted into a greater dimension, a powerful new place of Be-ing.

Enter the place where habits do not exist, where you are 73 completely free in Me. Be free in the creative essence of Be-ing. This is enlightenment. The creative order of the mind and the heart.

I walk free in you as your Undying Self. The rhythm of My 74 heartbeat becomes yours. We are poised together—you and I—in oneness. And we walk together. We are unified as the GodSelf.

Walk Free

Cast off the old rags of habit. Walk free! Each moment is 75 sparkling new with vital realizations and revelations. New ideas spiral out of old thought forms and patterns as you live in Me. You are bound no longer. The rhythm is the GodSelf. Align and be. My home is with you. And your home is in Me.

Live not to worship Me but to know Me in your heart as 76 your rhythm, your mind, your identity as truth. I AM the GodSelf. In essence I AM you.

CHAPTER TWENTY-EIGHT

Peace

Let each moment of your life expression 1
here on this earth
be a tribute to God: an anthem of peace.

Therefore, show not the way, but be it. 2
In being it others will follow.
Peace is not something found. It is.

In the flow of My Spirit you find perfect peace. I AM 3
peace. You cannot make peace. When you loose all
attachments, you will find peace. Remember I said, "Your
world is not My world?" It is so. As you learn to abide in Me,
My world becomes your world, infinite peace.

✦ True peace is not deserved nor attained. It *is*. 4

✦ Receive Me, your divinity, and let Me live. I AM waves 5
of Intelligence always conscious of Myself as truth.
In Me you will be at peace.

✦ Peace surrounds you: the eternal peace of the Creator. 6
It is this peace that is the creative substance of
your life.

✦ You do not have to look for peace. It is always with 7
you as My life.

✦ See through arguments and conflicts and wars. I AM 8
the peace you seek.

✦ Once you become conscious of the peace I AM, 9
nothing can disturb you nor take the peace from you.

I offer you peace: the peace of divine understanding, the 10
peace of rebirth into Me. Peace is your awareness in the stillness
of My being. You have but to call on Me and peace will come.
A surrendered soul rests in peace.

Be at peace with yourself. Know that I AM in your day as 11
your whole day complete and perfect. The day radiates out
from the peaceful heart at rest in Me. When you let the day
come through you as God in manifestation, your soul is at
rest and abundant.

In God you will find your peace and through God you will 12
know peace in all the earth.

I Have A
Plan For
Each One
Of You

Stay steady in the storm; creative power can create a "storm" 13
as it swirls and forms its creation. As you can remain calm in
the midst of Me forming of Myself, so you are ready to march
ahead into new aspects of Creative Fire. Set your sights to
this place. Knowing we are One causes union of all life. It
creates an impetus for creation, and it is the very method I
use to create My universes.

When you activate My Creative Force you have 14
responsibilities, for you are set upon a new place of Action
and Reaction. If you know "The Lord's Prayer,"[1] use it. You
will find great power of stabilization within this prayer.

Peace Is
Ordered
From
Within

Every quarrel and disagreement is resolved as you stabilize in 15
your Christ Center. I AM the peace that passes understanding.
I AM stabilized emotion in the heart. I AM the presence of
God. Come to the peace of God within your own heart and
that peace will objectify as your experience.

As you return "home," Oneness gives of Itself. The balance 16
of life is there in the Oneness that is the Omnipresence of
Being. This balance is *with you* and is your experience. Carry
this consciousness into the battlefield and there will be no
battlefield. You have but to release your consciousness into
the One. There AM I. All must come back to One. This is the

---

[1] See Matthew 6:9-13.

emergence. Then I can be. I AM the perfect equation within you.

Peace is. By the very act of centering, you have entered a 17 new dimension of mind and body. From the Innermost Heart God takes expression immediately. *All things must come home to the One. Then I AM that which appears.* I AM in expression. In this altered frequency of creative power, unity is vitalized. The program of peace is now on the planet and it is *nourished and sustained* by you. You are the most important person on earth at this moment.

Divine Love restores the frequency and consummates the 18 peace of I AM THAT I AM. You have roots that you know not of. Keep digging! Love dissolves the quarrel, the false appearance, for there is only one, and I AM That! Here you have the secret of how the creative power, completely stabilized, rises in partnership with the GodSelf. In this powerful and creative blending, this power is activated and rises into expression *as instant manifestation.*

Peace On   As you align with the Center of your own being, you will 19
Earth   draw those of like mind.

As you work in tune with My rhythms on earth, you will 20 find the peace you seek in all efforts, be they large or small. Our life is together.

Peace does not have its preferences. There are no victors in 21 peace. Peace is.

Release all sense of conflict to Me. Become conscious of 22 the one Source. Where I AM there is no confusion, no doubt. *Conflict comes from a disagreement with My reality. Be conscious of Me and all conflict dissolves.* This is true for your whole planet. You can live in peace with one another when you allow Me—the Divine Presence—to attend to your needs. Contemplate this for it is so.

The God peace you seek is within yourself. Go there. Do 23 not battle an untruth. Be at peace within yourself.

Consciousness must rise out of the battlefield into the Garden of Eden, the stabilized center where I AM. Such a stabilization of forces can and will cause change to the planet. Center on the unity of all peoples everywhere. The vision of light and love is within your heart and soul. When you know the Truth all else is affected. Realize the Truth for all your brothers and sisters. Let your consciousness rest in Me.

What It Is To Be Peaceful
The peaceful brother or sister is the one who practices 24 nonviolence in his, her life. He or she carries no thought of disturbance in the heart. He or she knows the Truth and the planet is strengthened by this knowing. In this knowing, many are blessed and true form takes its place on earth. This is the settlement of the new skies, and this is the graduation into a new frequency where stars can rekindle themselves in the Flame of Christ.

Never forget that a real and true relationship is born of 25 God, not of men. In the flow of Being all humanity is at one. My Spirit burns brightly and in harmony with all life. Nothing is apart from Me. As you understand this Truth, that there is no error in Me, all life is with you.

Loving expression is determined by your rhythm. There 26 are no enemies in oneness. Divide not. Consciousness divides not itself from its creation. It determines it.

Graduation Is Near
Many changes are taking place on this planet. It is part of a 27 rapid push forward into a new paradigm. The shift is at hand. It is imminent.

In the presence of My Central Headquarters of Love and 28 Light all is in harmony with the Father's rhythms. Through this Gateway shall you enter, through this alignment shall you go. And as you do, many shall be given new assignments and rhythms to qualify.

As your Creator emerges *as Self-Government* on this planet, 29 those of you who are receptive shall be gathered into a life circuit of My own. This powerful circuit known as the Christ Body is a new system whereupon you, as System Sovereign headquarters frequency, shall foster a love of Christ never experienced before on this planet, or any planet of your system. A new order is coming to Earth by My hand. I welcome you as part of this new government.

Have the trust to understand that "I AM" the government 30 of all nations and I govern well. You, the Seed of God emerged, translate out of a consciousness of limitation and selfishness into *living light*. A supreme existence is yours as you permit the Christed Seed, your GodSelf, to emerge and live.

Come Into Peace The peace that you seek is within you. The heart carries it. 31 I have established My peace even before creation. I AM at peace with Myself.

The coming of the Lord is peace. It is the presence of peace 32 in your system.

The coming of the new world of light is indeed peace.   33

Think upon these things. I have need of your awareness.   34

CHAPTER TWENTY-NINE

Love Is Consciousness Divine

I have love for all life　　　　　　　　　　　　　　1
and if you do not have it also,
we are not one.

The God Consciousness moves　　　　　　　　　　2
in waves of love.

Begin each day with love. Love is the generation of My　3
Spirit. It is the purity of My motion. It is the presence of
My Creative Power in you. It is My abundance. Without love
you cannot create. It is the substance from which I know
Myself as your Christ Center. As love I contain the universe.
The universe was founded in love.

To know love is to know God. I AM the omnipresence of　4
love in you. Receive My love and give it forth even as it is
received. You cannot stop love from giving of itself. It is the
master plan of the universe. Stand with Me and love with Me,
for are we not one?

Internal organs feed on love. Your body can be nourished　5
by love. Just as My universe is vitalized by love, so might your
physical body be divinely nourished with infinite love. In robes
of splendor I dress you. I AM always present. Deny Me not.
If you deny Me you cannot benefit from My giving presence.
Where I AM there is love.

**Will You
Accept Me**

Mortals very often say they love, but they do not. This is 6 because mortals very often claim people and possess them. They say this is love. But it is not. Possession is not love. There are no boundaries in Me. To free is to love.

God is love. To be receptive to love is to be open to receive 7 the abundant life. The *willingness to receive* opens you to the infinite Being I AM. You and I are one whole Be-ing.

You are created in My image and likeness as I AM. Together 8 we are love. The love that I have for you in Me is divine substance; it is the creative element and tissue that feeds and clothes you. As the Life Energy I AM pours through you, see that Energy, divine in its origin and present in you, as your universal supply. Love is the very basis of all life energy. It is the presence of the Creator in you.

Nothing must be issued or decreed without love. My Spirit 9 rests in love.

**The Test
Of Love**

Emotional purity is found in the outpouring of your 10 Christed Energy: this is the open heart. Let the flow of My precious love be in you, the rhythm of joy everlasting. This love I AM centers itself in creation, forgiving all. That is why I say there is no karma in Me. My activity is love. As I restore My Earth by love, so I call you into this love.

My love is universal. It is for every human being. 11 I touch and restore all life by My love. In this love is the presence of God. Love is not a feeling, it is beingness. It reaches out to all people everywhere and welcomes them back into the heart of God. I have no memory. I do not forgive and forget. I know only good and I AM at rest in that.

**Application
Of The
Power
"To Be"**

To love *with the Creator* vitalizes every membrane of your 12 being, enabling you to finalize and go forward as a light upon this Earth, a powerful Christ presence. When you have this kind of love there is nothing that is denied you. *The creative*

power in you knows itself as you and permits itself to be used by
you as love. This generates a new system and a new creation.

Believe in the Christ within you as the divine love force 13
and form from That. The perfect ministry of the Christ is the
open heart. It takes courage to love in such a way, as the
master Jesus demonstrated. Be loving, and love will greet you
everywhere you go. It cannot help but do so for it is your
love as expression, and it is your consciousness in
manifestation.

What Is You will adjust to these new feelings of impersonal love as 14
Impersonal your consciousness unfolds. Attachments will drop away and
Love you will be universally aware. When you are cleansed of all
personal feeling—that of attachment and possession—you are
apt to have a sense of emptiness and fulfillment. It is necessary
to purify to discover this perfect love that is My Spirit inside
yourself. From the emptiness comes fulfillment. True
emptiness calls to be fulfilled by the glory of God. As you
position yourself in emptiness you know you shall be fulfilled.

You are not without love. The purification leads to 15
resurrection and the fulfillment of the Creator in you. It is
time to cross over into a new dimension. This does not mean
that this is the end of marriage or companionship. However
it does mean that you are in a different sphere where you are
not encumbered with the personal attachments of the "lower
self." *There is no ownership in love.* This new dimension is
Christ's dimension where dwells the Creator as love.

Nothing When you carry love in its fullness, in its richness, you carry 16
But Love the Christ, who is *Christed Energy.* It is the same. That is why
the New Testament is so radically different from the Old
Testament.

Once the soul dies to mortal sense (we are all caught up in 17
fields of our own creation), the soul rests in love. Where love
is, I AM. This is an atomic field of Divine Intelligence.

I AM, as love, is the stabilization core of the Universe. It is 18 the heart-form.

Let Me love you as My Son. As you give yourself entirely 19 to Me, I fill you with love. As you are filled with love so shall My universe be bathed in it also. Every time I touch you I touch all.

You are on the plane of omnipresent love that is the Creator 20 in expression. Flesh and blood of Me, allow Me to love unequivocally without margins, boundaries or definitions. I AM love itself, AM I not?

When darkness comes, then you must love and it will be 21 light again. Love is the cohesive power of the Universe. It connects one to another and is always in motion as truth.

Take no enemies. I have no enemy in Me. Do not fight 22 back. Turn the other cheek. Lift up your heart and love; allow Me to love as I AM. Respond to every action with love. This is your safeguard as well as your protector. For love forms a shield of itself. Nothing can penetrate through this shield save love, a love that is given without thought of self.

Only in love can you conquer the last enemy called "death." 23 Only in love will you know peace. You have entered a new dimension. This place is the revelation of the soul in love. The power of this revelation knows no bounds.

Animals Are Your Brothers
In the days to come, you will learn of My Word in a new 24 and different way. Animals will go free once again. They will serve humanity and all creation in new and different ways. They will joy with you. And they will have My blessing which is given upon all.

Animals are not to be eaten. They are given to you as 25 companions. Just as you have elder brothers and sisters who assist you in your spiritual understanding, so are you to assist your brothers and sisters in the animal kingdom. They walk with you. You will be judged by your treatment of them. They come not to be eaten but to grow with you. When you understand this there will be no war.

My animals are My expression even as you are. As you see 26 God in them, you lift them, even as I have lifted you. My animals are forming a greater bond with humanity. And even as you ascend to higher vibration and new dimensions of idea, so shall My animal kingdom.

Turn Not Away Enter each day with an open heart, in thanksgiving. I AM 27 revelation throughout the day. Let Me flow! My day is filled with love, light and laughter.

Anticipate each day with a grateful heart. Expect the day 28 to be "fruitful," as all days come into fruition as My Being. How plenteous My supply is when you love! Be blessed in the day and live each precious hour, every minute, in the love essence I AM.

And as a final thought for you: I want you to always 29 remember I *want* to give to you. I *desire* to express as love and light. My Spirit is here for you to unite with, to connect with, to create with. This is the key to your future on this planet and the many planets to come.

CHAPTER THIRTY

Emotion Is Power

Transform your emotions. Your emotions are My energy in motion.   1
They become the creative power from which all things are made.

Let every emotion be transfigured by love.   2
As you do this, your spiritual identity flows forth into creative substance.
Through love all things are made aright.

Within the temple of God, e-motion (energy in motion)   3
is the creative fire, rising to behold itself as life
intended. *That is its intent.* Any obstruction to this
can cause serious disability. Let your emotions be of
gratitude, praise and love. As you magnify the Christ
expression in your heart, we will be able to move as
one body and manifest upon this earth vibrant energy of
pure love and life. This will be the new consciousness
of man. We will work together, you and I, at one. God and
man in harmony.

Trans-formation Of Your Emotions   Emotions rise to express My word. That is what praise is all   4
about! The grateful heart is always answered. When
despondent, praise God. Be thankful. Delight in welcoming
God into your heart and there let the God peace transform
all emotional upheaval into the Christ purpose.

    The act of thankfulness and gratitude to the Creator of all   5
life brings happiness to the system. Ask to serve. How can I
best serve you, Lord? And God within you will answer. When
you lose your life to the Spirit of God, you will find your life
in oneness with all that is. Give back to God the life that you
think is yours alone, and mighty will your life be! You will be

the light of the world and you will honor the Father and the Mother in the embodiment of Christ.

Return your emotions to the GodSelf and become a 6 powerful person in the Lord. When you release your base emotions to your GodSelf, you become the creative power and you are truly aligned with the forces that Be.

The Rhythm Of The Creator

I have but to say something for it to be. Thus all life lives on 7 My breath. I AM your desire in fulfillment. I AM your creative power emerging. And I AM that which is formed of Me in perfect vibration of agreement.

Let your mind be at one with My Mind. Be raised into the 8 consciousness of one mind, the Universal and Divine Mind of truth and light. When you are at rest in Divine Mind, all thoughts come from *the Originator of All Life.*

I know you as My perfect expression. In Me you have life. 9 Live in the past no longer. If you continue to draw on the past, then shall you reap that which is of that past. *Be conscious of the present moment.* For I say I AM That which is present. I AM ready to form of Myself.[1]

The children of the light are expressions of My own Be- 10 ing. I remember them in Me as I AM. Thus I empower them. They are conscious of Me and I of them. We are one.

All I AM is Consciousness in declared position. There is no 11 other life but this. Come to your own radiance and be with Me. I call you forth as My divine expression: *the I AM.*

Give Me your emotions that I may empower them to create 12 new worlds of perfect love and benevolent light. I speak as your own declared Christhood. We are one in manifest energy. What Jesus knew when he walked this earth, you know also. It is in your genes. Be conscious of this. Let go of the lost and unfriendly, for I AM not of that.

---

[1] In fact I AM already formed. When desire originates from the higher self, it means that the creative power bears notice that the perfect form—be it increased financial abundance, a new scientific discovery, a peaceful resolution to conflict—is formed in the etheric and ready to objectify if you agree. Desire, however, without the basis of this unified agreement between human and divine is causeless, and without the support of the Great and Mighty Council. Therefore, it is useless.

**The Trans-
formation
Of Your
Energy**

True emotion walks with a clean heart: it carries the 13
divine desire. True emotion lifts itself into the Creative
Spirit. Emotion, when faithfully carried, benefits all life.
It is the creative substance—the divine fire of life—when
purified. Contact the Christ presence within your heart.
Request that all emotion be purified, lifted in praise
and in love for all life. When emotions are purified, ego has
no part.

God releases Himself through the emotions, purified 14
substance, and forms *of Himself* that which is decreed and
registered as your desire and Christ intention. When there is
no motive but selfless giving, God truth is on the field. You
are then emotionally stable and ready to serve the Master and
the World Plan.

**The
Emotional
Power Of
The
Universe**

Once stabilized, emotional power is the Universe Creator 15
in motion. It is the creative process as Divine Will. God
centered, you will always work with your emotions for divine
good. Your emotions, as you release them to the higher intent,
will come under the jurisdiction of the GodSelf who you are
in truth.

When you release the emotions willingly into God intent— 16
it is the willingness that pleases Me—you are raising the
creative power or kundalini. As you permit and so decree all
your emotion into the GodSelf, this divine energy is then
empowered as My Daughter, the Creative Spirit.

Just as I have a Son, I have a Daughter. One is not without 17
the other in My creative flame of Being. My expression
demands both polarities to rhythmically express Me as I AM.
And as you dedicate and commit the *feeling* process, all your
hopes and desires, into the GodSelf, I express as unified Being.
I AM the Creator, then, in My creation. It is then that no
desire is without Me. I be-come what I AM. This is the purified
entrance of My power into you as the I AM Consciousness. It
is the Christ.

The power of My wish is determined by your receptivity 18 put in motion by your desire. What you are conscious of, you become. Your emotional reaction and intensity will steer Divine Thought into manifest form. It will drive form or idea into being.

My Son's[2] life as you is as My nest. I long for that place in 19 you so that I might be. So, as I speak of the creative force in you, I ask you not to draw back but to believe in the wondrous gift I have in you as "I AM." Come into the temple of Being. Come in and partake of the creative power, the power that is the God-Force in you. Rise to your greater part!

The creative power is the capstone. This power that I speak 20 of is the female pole risen: the Christed Eve or the new Eve. Thus the feminine side of the Christ is revealed. When you release to Me all desire and return your emotions to Me, I become the Thought-Guardian of your soul, the reason for your desire. My activity becomes your activity. We are one vibration and one in motion. To live in this way is peace. And darkness is no more.

It is through *your feelings* I must express. Releasing your 21 energy into Me allows this expression of My being (I AM THAT I AM) to fully realize Itself. The I AM presence or the GodSelf becomes the power within you; and it is by this power that I AM able to thrust My Self forth into expression *as I AM.* You willingly permit Me *to desire* through you. What a powerful instrument you become! We are One and we function together as one being. Through body, mind and spirit I AM. This is the Presence of God or Truth in Its full expression to be. It is the God Son.

I AM The Daughter Also   I have given you My Son. Now I wish to give you My 22 Daughter, as She is the power within you. She is the Creative Spirit. *She is the vibrant current of My Being. I think and She carries My thought and it becomes the Word.*

---

[2] The embodiment of the I AM. The word Son here denotes the GodSelf or the partnership of both God and man as one. This is the true Son of creation.

Thus the risen Eve, who is My Daughter in you, is the 23
vibration of light and life.

As Within,   Thought and feeling are one in unified intelligence. When 24
So Without they are joined, thought and feeling embody the creative act
of Will, the full intent of the Creator. I store My intent in you
to be accepted.

When you have received My desire in you and agree with 25
that desire, My Daughter in you (as the risen Eve or feminine
pole) *will objectify* the desire into form. *Every decree that is of
Me is fulfilled.* That fulfillment is your answer to the problem,
the need manifest, the Word conceived.

As the creative power rises in your awareness, to be known 26
and understood, that power will serve the Creator. It will not
serve any other medium. Come home into My sacred body
of Being. I AM the Garden of Eden in you when the oneness
is proclaimed. The Garden of Eden is discovered to be
conscious union with God. Man and woman stand together
as two-in-one in harmony with My Inner Voice. And the two,
emotion and thought, are joined in agreement to manifest
the Creative Intent.

Go Empty   When you have emptied yourself of all lust and selfish will, 27
I, the Christ within as the I AM, can move through you into
expression. It is then the journey becomes light. And all
abundance is yours. There is no physical effort. *I have come.*

Fulfillment is your consciousness and My consciousness at 28
one. The creative energy—My Spirit—must fill you to fulfill
you. This act of My creative energy as it embodies itself is My
Word. When emotions are raised into light, the presence of
God is present as the Will and Intent. Subject to one Will,
there is nothing that can harm you. No thing can deter you
from the full expression I AM. In God's will you have the
LAW on your side. You are the Word and you function
that way.

It is My full intention to bring all back unto Me.   29

I AM omnipresent, omniscient and omnipotent. My 30
Consciousness is the Creator.

As you become at one with My will, there is no other.   31

CHAPTER THIRTY-ONE

God Seeks to Fulfill

Fulfillment is the vibration of complete embodiment of Me in you.   1
You cannot be fulfilled without Me. I AM all.

I n God you live and have your being. The awakening to   2
this reality is the spiritual journey.

Direct Mani-festation   Speaking into creation decreed Intelligence, units of My   3
own Life Energy, causes creation to objectify in My image
and likeness.

When I—the I AM Presence—decree, *I AM like the*   4
creation. We are as one. You have but to seek the sacred
Light within you and let that sacred Light decree. I fill
you with My nature to objectify as I AM. I AM the Creator
and the created.

The fulfillment felt by being in the One, and permitting   5
the creative process (I AM THAT I AM) to embody, is the
formation of the manifestation. Fulfillment is the
manifestation. It tells you that you have decreed aright. Listen
to the still, small Voice in you. It knows the way. It is the
Creator emerged.

When you release the energy-in-motion up into the creative   6
self I AM, you restore My creation to its rightful place and
give birth to new objects of My rhythm and creative structure.
You multiply.

Serving The Christ   Your emotions are sacred. They are creative energy, the   7
fluid of My Being. Accept your emotions as My living fire-
expression of God in you. Respect them. Care for them. They
enunciate the tone and the quality of My Being.

Emotion is the presence of the Divine Mother. Emotion as 8
divine fire of love carries the Christ and distributes It. Emotion
has a mission to qualify itself as living light: the intensity of
the Christ expression.

All emotion must return to the GodSelf *as Life* 9
Energy and there serve the supreme master of all
creation.

The powerful forces of emotion rest largely in the woman. 10
She is the nesting place for the creative power. She distributes
her power through the light. When you ill-treat the feminine
position, you cause imbalance in your life and in your body
itself. The power of the female pole is rarely understood. Yet
all must return to the original creation of perfect love. The
Son must find the Daughter. Together they will govern in
perfect order of divine love.

When the emotions are in agreement with the Divine Will 11
and in tune with the Cosmic Lift, so they vitalize what is
termed the Creative Daughter in our planetary system.

The incoming spiraling force, known as the Creative 12
Daughter or Spirit, is the presence of Christ Intelligence and
the power of unified creation.

Woman Out In the qualifying of energy and the release of the old world, 13
Of Bondage the woman returns to her divine nature. God's pure life is
released through woman.

As you reflect and restore the feminine pole 14
within yourself, the effect on your system will
be creative and empowering.

Woman is to find herself in Me and there receive her true 15
self as light. In this place, the woman is the Creative Principle
in Me. Understanding this, woman must decide at this time
whom she will obey. If she chooses Me, her GodSelf, she will

know and understand great power. She will vibrate that power and demonstrate it in the harmony of My Word. Servant no longer, she will move quickly into a place of authority with Me. This completes the woman in Me and restores the rightful rhythm on earth.

The Risen Eve

As you become aware of the supreme position of woman, 16 your female pole will rise as divine authority. A release will be felt within you—be you woman or man in form—and you will have the ability to come and go and to command with full authority in Me.

How you treat the woman in you is important. How you 17 treat the woman in your life is equally important. How you, woman, treat yourself will call new creation into being. As you realize that the feminine or woman is one with God, so must the emotions, founded in God's rhythm as My Spirit, also be one with God. They cannot be separated.

When emotions are allowed free rein, they can be 18 destructive. With the increase of creative power on earth, these forces called "emotion" can be destructive. They must become the risen Eve!

The sacred, divine power within you is to be returned to 19 the GodSelf. In this way do emotions and feeling receive My full attention as light, or ascended vibration.

True power is creative. Returned to the God Center, you 20 may decree and your words will be heard and they will take form.

Something To Think About

To release the woman (womb-man or subconscious mind) 21 to your GodSelf is to enter the superconscious mind (risen Eve). The subconscious ascends to the superconscious, just as kundalini (creative energy) flows upward through the spine to the place of awareness: the crown center or chakra. There is no subconscious then; enlightenment occurs. *One knows.* It is in this place the human becomes divine or sun/son of

God and triumphs over matter. Here man or consciousness lives as the full enlightened Self, a bright and glorious sun. The subconscious has entered the conscious state of awareness. To bring this to your awareness, concentrate on the presence of the Christ Self. Let the consciousness of God pass through your system. This is the way to Truth on this planet.

I Have A Mission For Your Emotion

You see, emotion cannot give itself away idly. *It is creative.* 22 In its oneness (total agreement) with thought, the word will manifest as decreed.

The holy mission of your emotion is to birth the Son of 23 your own consciousness. It is to bring into fruition your inner Child, that which you are in God's Word. When you let your emotion rise in praise and gratitude, it will do this.

Honor your emotions. The more you honor and commit 24 your emotions to God, the more light is vitalized and actualized. Until there is nothing but the light of the divine Self, carried by the Holy Spirit as creative power, your emotions will be nonproductive and without authority.

Be At Peace

A calm mind produces good results. When the emotions 25 are at rest in the Spirit, then you have the creative power in position to produce of itself. This is the divine secret of creation. My vital issue, My life energy, is within you as you decree My word, My wishes, as divine expression I AM. Once stabilized, My vital force becomes your vital force. (When you are anxious or worry about yourself, I cannot help you. You have committed your emotions to the lower field of desire where I AM not. You must lift your thoughts to Me. I stand ready to be.)

When you consciously realize your oneness with all life, 26 you are released from all emotional trauma. Energy moves in its correct balance—unhindered—and expresses as divine love throughout all creation. Fear, depression and other emotional problems are linked to lack of awareness. Once you are consciously aware of your life as the GodSelf, you awaken and become consciously aware of your birthright. You are the light of the world.

Contact your inner Being and be quiet. Rejoice that you 27 are in Me and I in you. Give up the struggle. Let go. I will take over your life, if you will let Me. I AM the whole and the completeness and the fulfilling light of your GodSelf. Stand with Me.

Hear the Word of divine intelligence as It is sounded on 28 the Breath. It is good. It is pure. Struggle not. Listen. Darkness will melt away in the healing vibration of Truth. Healing power in this Voice will quiet your emotions. Behold the Life within your heart, and the storm is quieted.

Just One Power

✧ No longer does emotion rule you, you are one with 29 emotion and that emotion is spiritual energy glorifying God.

✧ You are one with the creative power and at home in 30 it. It does not use you. You are one with it.

✧ Just as you ride a good stallion in complete harmony, 31 so you vibrate at one with the power of God and ideas flow to you to manifest.

✧ You command this power into expression as I AM 32 THAT I AM. And the command that you vibrate into life after the Order of Melchizedek originates from your God Center and is perfect in its agreement with all life.

✧ Though the unruly emotions may tremble, stand in 33 the divine authority of light, knowing with Jesus: "Peace, be still!" With the words of the Lord shall you speak and even as he did, so shall you.

✧ Quiet the emotions with My Sword of Truth.   34

If or when you find that you have lost control of your 35 emotions, return "home." Release into the light of My

Consciousness any hurt or pain you are feeling. I embody as love. Let go and let love in.

All disorder is caused by lack of surrender. Surrender to 36 God draws you into the Christ Flame where perfect, holy order dwells. There is no disorder in Me. From your Christ within, only unity, divine harmony and perfect alignment can vibrate as the living Word.

Your base and negative emotional reactions are not 37 important to Me. Give Me something I can use! If or when you find that you have lost control of your emotions, return to your God Center, the Christ within. There, in that place of light and harmlessness, all energy-in-motion is reseeded into love.

Enter The Heart

What you have forgiven never returns.   38

To forgive another is to forgive yourself. This power of 39 forgiveness returns you to the heart, home of your divinity. If you can forgive all those who have hurt you *and love them,* then there is no karma, no debt to pay, no lesson to be learned. The heart is the place of *willingness* to love. I store My love in your heart.

As you enter the heart, you make contact with the Christ, 40 the powerful and now dominant energy of compassion. This Christ Center, once opened, will vibrate divine grace within your system. *It always realigns the forces of appearance.* The gateway to the GodSelf is the heart.

Bring your emotions into the heart. Let the heart love. So 41 many choke off love by their resistance to it. Let My Heart shine out as fulfilled emotion, as energy not wasted but restored to its rightful place in Me. *What you give Me, I will use.* Emotion offered up to God manifests as Holy Spirit, the divine light of creation.

An emotional problem signifies that you have not offered 42 up the emotions, not allowed the emotions to rise for positive creative purposes. Let your emotions shift to the creative power. It is the nature of God to fulfill your mission on earth.

Love Is The Only Power Not only must your thought be pure and loving, but your 43 feelings be dedicated and *committed* to God's expression. For the Will of God must be manifest in feelings as well as thought. You are My manifest expression.

If you react negatively to a given situation, you breathe in 44 this energy and it will manifest. You have decreed negativity into your life. Thus it must manifest by your decree. Be the commander of your emotions. Human emotion must not be thrown about, for your emotions are as energy that must serve the universal good. Know the truth of your embodiment. Listen to the Creator within you. Be willing to listen, for I will speak of divine intent.

The vibration of love, which is order flowing through your 45 soul, is the active creator. As you meet situation after situation with love, there can be no thing that will harm you while you love. *Put on the whole armour of God.* (Ephesians 6:11) *For God is love.* (I John 4:8)

Wonderful Thoughts to Think About

1) Do not return negative with negative.

2) Foster love wherever you go.

3) Direct all energy-in-motion into love's gate.

4) Meet error with love and you cannot be affected by external conditions of the negative.

5) Where there is love, there is no evil.

6) Love declares its divinity in itself.

7) The only true religion is love.

8) God is love, an untroubled, unbroken unity of Spirit energy that announces Itself by Its purity and dissolves all iniquities in Its path.

9) In the love I have for My creation I AM.

10) Divine love knows no boundaries.

11) Love is the only power. Remember that. It is the gateway to paradise.

12) To know love is to know your Son's life in you. It is the omnipresent Christ. I AM love.

13) God fulfills you by His love.

CHAPTER THIRTY-TWO

Claim Harmony

Only true harmony can exist as life intended.   1
It is the song of God and the realm of the master.

E motional control is to be harvested. The Christ is the   2
control center: the place of reality and creative power,
the place where *I AM*.[1] This Christ Center rests in the heart.

The creative power stirs and embodies itself as it hears or   3
recognizes the perfect vibration "I AM." The God Power
responds to the oneness of God Consciousness. Once the
stabilized creative power, My Spirit, recognizes My Voice in
you, it will always answer by *immediate creation*. This is the
Law of Life. There is only harmony in My will.

Once emotion is quieted, the creative power takes root. It   4
will thrust itself up into the heart and beyond to show itself
as light. This creative power, once it is shown as the Sun,
light from within, is the emergence. When all emotion is
restored to the Spirit of God, then the Holy Spirit returns to
live with you. Your energy-in-motion, when transformed into
living light or Christed energy, becomes the divine power of
God: the infinite power of love and light.

The creative power always carries the I AM Presence within   5
itself. It vibrates I AM out of Itself. When that power as the
"I AM" is felt within the universe, there is instant creation.
Let this be understood: what humanity faces now is
magnificent creative potential.

I would not have you poor nor suffering. The Consciousness I   6
AM permits only divine Be-ing out-picturing as "I."

---

[1] Remember that the word "I AM" is the union of man and God at one. When this union as
agreement flashes, the creative power immediately out-pictures that which is spoken. This
power circuit is called the Melchizedek power. Jesus brought that to earth.

**Release
And Reap**

✧ Anticipate the good in your life. It will manifest. 7

✧ Know that I AM all good and I AM waiting to show 8
you who I AM in your life. As you let Me into your
life as you, I will easily return to you all that I AM.

✧ My Consciousness is your consciousness in the One. 9
That is the Kingdom. It is what "returning home to
the Father's house" really means.

✧ Let go of all your possessions. You possess nothing 10
in Me. You don't need possessions, nor do you need
to possess. I AM everything in perfect harmony and
rhythm. I AM not separate from life. *I AM life.* AM
I not wonderful?

✧ As you release, so are you released. And chains fall 11
away. Release your identity also. Find Me in you as
your identity. This is "I AM."

✧ I have a great harvest for you as you come Home. 12
When you can release to Me all things that you have
held close, so AM I able to release to you all that I
have in Me for you to enjoy. Balance is obtained and
maintained by releasing into God all your
attachments.

**Shake The
Dust From
Your Feet**

Do not look back. When you accept the Christ as your 13
true Self, you must also accept the purity that is the Truth
flowing through you into expression now. This purity of Truth
is called "I AM."

The very breath you take is the breath of God. You are 14
swept up into the one identity. You are formed of Me. Nothing
is kept from you. You can have everything.

As attachments fall away, so must the world as you have 15
known it. Your consciousness now belongs with Me and I
with you. We are One.

The Christ Center is within your heart. As your undivided 16
attention goes into that Center and receives it, that unity of

identity will release you from all entanglements, chains, oaths
and vows. You are free in Me. I come to claim My own. If
there is addiction, I will thrust that from you. But remember
to give Me the power. In giving Me the power, that which is
not of Me departs.

> I release you of that which has gone before *as*   17
> *you release yourself.* If you do not release yourself,
> I cannot help you. Shake the dust from your feet
> and come follow Me. I AM not subject to
> punishment.

Remember not to look back. I seek not to lift you out of 18
something but rather to know you consciously in Me as *I*.
For in this way is the worldly consciousness thrust aside and
conscious union with God achieved.

I AM That   You know who you are: the light of My own being as I. Do 19
I AM   not attach to that which is leaving you. Stay centered by
knowing God in you. All else leaves for lack of power, for lack
of energy, for lack of belief.

It is when you become attached to a thought form, a pattern 20
of existence, a person, place or thing, that you become subject
to that attachment, often confused and lost within it. Think
about "the fall" and what that really means. Your freedom is
in the God Center, in the Creator Son.

The Divine   I give you Omnipresence: the divine Kingdom of God. Seek 21
Impulse   My Word, My Consciousness in direct energy flow. When
you do this, you will see the vibrations change in your life.

In My Spirit dwell. I will motivate you. Seek no goals other 22
than the goal of the heart. This goal objectifies *as the living
Word* with the Breath of Creation. There is much fruit upon
the limb, but you must breathe it through and give flesh and
blood to it. That is what is meant by the words, "Go forth

and multiply." The "fast-food" fantasy teachings of human desire fall away in the wholeness of My reality in you.

Consciousness is breathing creatively, constantly, releasing 23 divine life throughout the cosmos. My fire of life is *with you.* I will motivate you.

Nothing is too complicated that Divine Mind cannot 24 resolve. All things are made in Me. What is not made is not real. Rest in the wholeness.

Depend upon the Source of all supply. When weakness 25 comes over you, return to beingness. Breathe the one life.

You must be willing to turn to Me, the I AM Presence, at 26 all times. I will be with you. I will be there.

I cannot help you if you are not *with* Me. Did it ever occur 27 to you that I might very well create the feeling of weakness so that you would return to Me as the Source of all life?

Consciously know the source of your supply. Let the rhythm 28 proclaim itself. All life is good in Me. See and believe in My goodness before it appears and say "Thank you." *I must come to the grateful heart.* My divine impulse is to be with you.

Fear Not   What you fear is never real. It cannot stand. It has no power 29 in Me. Reality is God, love, perfection, divine order. When you give power to disorder, you create it. Take the power away from the appearance. Give Me the power in your life. The instant you do this, new life appears.

That which is false and untrue has no life lest you give it 30 life by your belief in it. Quiet yourself and be. Let your whole be-ing return to God. *I AM the perfect order of your being.*

Stand in God awareness as peace and know that, as you do, 31 peace is released as My Being. Look not to the outer appearance. Give Me the power. Let peace be. Then harmony will be established in your life.

Remember, energy that is restricted, that cannot expand 32 into expression of the GodSelf, becomes destructive. Detach from your fear as you faithfully affirm I AM. Allow Me to express through you. As your state of awareness expands, you will know and feel we are one. Let Me, the inner dimension of the real you, the constancy of fire and love, express outwardly as your heart's desire fulfilling your mission and My mission on earth.

CHAPTER THIRTY-THREE

Home in Light

You were conceived in light.   1
Through your GodSelf you must be the light.

W hen you turn inward to Me, I begin to vibrate through   2
you as creative power, the life energy I AM. It is this
positive thrust of emotion into the fire of love and light that
causes *instant creation.*

The power of this thrust cannot be contained within an   3
ordinary human body. Thus I AM contained in a body of light
that is the body of My Consciousness over yours. This is a
body that is forthcoming to the human race. It is the Sun.

I AM ready to reserve this body in your name if you, in   4
turn, will give Me your emotion. It is this energy-in-motion
that is destined to come home in light. As the Sun-body, we
are one unit of Me, the GodSelf.

Be Prepared   As you return your emotions to Me, I cancel all negativity   5
and I transform these emotions into light. Let Me, the Christ
within your heart, balance your emotions into creative power
and let Me drive those emotions upward into light! God needs
you even as you need God. I created the need in you that *I*
might be.

The passage of your energies through your heart and   6
through your head centers qualifies you and lifts you into a
new realm of creativity and love. I have come that you might
have love and have it more abundantly.

Any time you feel emotional imbalance, let the fear out of   7
your system. Breathe it through. Give your fear to the light
that all might be reconciled in Me. Breathe with the Breath

of Life slowly and consciously. Darkness shall become light. But you must trust in Me.

You have fears of punishment, Earth-people, fears of Me. 8 Yet I AM a God of love. Where is the love in your system that you have fear? As you learn to rely more and more on your GodSelf, the living truth within you, the Temple will be built; it will be a body of light. Be lifted out of what is not. Believe in Me. My nature is of love, what is there to fear?

Perhaps you may say: I have realized Truth. But when I go 9 into the "world" I lose it! Why? And the answer I must give you is: Take the Truth with you. Walk in Truth. Vibrate Truth. Do not abandon Truth because you are walking in the street or working at your job. *Stay in Truth.*

You are not separate from the Creator. You are one with 10 Me. If you can walk in faith—in knowingness I AM—then shall I show you a world of light. You are blessed of My Being and I AM you. We are one. It is only when you separate from Me in your consciousness that you know fear. I dismantle fear in love.

I Will Come In Power

These are My Final Days: I have already realized them in 11 Me and now they must come forth *as a system of Intelligence on earth.* This is My presence embodying Itself. It is the Creator form in manifestation. I have brought this into fruition that I can realize you in Me.

I will come in vibrations of light. Angels will accompany 12 Me. And I will come in power. This power will reconcile creation. The force of My embodiment will be as a great wave of power never before felt on this earth. I describe this power now, for you will need to adjust to it and prepare yourself for the mighty wind. These lessons are issued as a preparation.

The power I speak of is very much like the final push of the 13 mother as the child is born. Such a mighty wind it will be that if you are not properly aligned, properly prepared, the forces summoned into expression may prove too much for the physical body as well as mind and heart.

Prepare yourself well for the "Second Coming." Emotions 14 overlaid with fear cannot make the transition. As I embody as the Supreme Lord (Word) of the planet, you and I are one in all avenues of My experience upon this earth. We have no distance between us.

A New Cycle   Position yourself in the Truth I have given you. Ride the 15 wave of Consciousness. It is My Supreme Being stabilizing and knowing Itself as God on earth. Sing of Me. I AM the peace you seek. I AM with you. Be anxious not. Relax and bear Me forth—just as a mother would her son. That part of you that may still be rebellious is only unharnessed spirit.

I prepare you well that you might sail forth on a journey of 16 light. I have detained you that you might first feel the foundation (Divine Principle) under your feet. I have reclothed you that you might be sturdy in My creative power and wise in it also. Seek Me out of yourself. I AM there.

You Will Never Go Hungry   Therefore take no thought for your self: what you should 17 eat and what you should drink. Rather forgive and let go. Enter the Self of Self and there give up all but My Being in you. I AM the one you seek.

Learning to release "self" into the One is the secret of 18 initiation. Every initiation will demand this of you. Let your consciousness absorb the Master. Give way to the Spirit. So shall you walk in light as the GodSelf. Then will your emotions be translated into power, the power of the Living Light.

CHAPTER THIRTY-FOUR

The Perfect Relationship

Establish your relationship with the God Presence.　　　　1
In this relationship you will have everything you need.

It is through the Oneness that all things emerge in harmony,　　2
in conscious accord with all life.

Y ou have no gift greater than My Life in you. Once you　3
find that Life, and it is closer than breathing, you dispel
darkness. The darkness has no life of its own. Unless you give
it life, darkness is nonexistent.

　　God in you as you is the greater part. It is the part decreed　4
from the beginning. It is the Christ celebrated in the manger
of love. It is the waking of the True Self, the Self I AM. All
power goes to this place in you as you take up the resurrection
and the life. It is here in this place that you perceive a new
identity which is God Be-ing, the embodiment of the I AM.

The Eternal　　Let God in you be the only relationship you seek. Seek no　5
Relationship other. The one that has God does not seek anything other
than That, for That completes Itself through all life in ways
most perfect and harmonious.

　　If you could but relate to God in you as all that you seek,　6
and be filled with that One, there would be deep satisfaction
in your soul. Did not the Master Jesus tell you, "But seek ye
first the kingdom of God, and his righteousness; and all these
things shall be added unto you"? (Matthew 6:33) Because in

companionship with God all things are made. Therefore, seek out your relationship with God (Truth) first. This will establish your alignment and from that point the embodiment of all relationships is formed.

God is the eternal relationship from which all relation is 7 governed.

When you know you are with God and God is with you, a 8 marriage is formed between Spirit and the flesh. There is a continuity of expression in everything you do.

In God Consciousness, you are complete. In your 9 fulfillment, all life is the reflection of that fulfillment. God wants you to look to Him first so that He can enrich your life. *I AM the Presence and the Power. True relationship comes from Me. I AM the One sought if you would but know this.*

Come To Me   Begin to relate to the Christ in you. That Christ in you will 10 form of Itself that which you need and require in your life on earth. I AM a repository for all good. Receive Me in you and I will be abundant. If you could but know your place in Me, you would know this.

Let your consciousness ascend to the Christ Center in you. 11 Let the Christ be your relationship. I will fulfill you, and in this fulfillment all is one. Here, woman and man are in complete accord. They do not battle one another; they cannot, for *I AM*.

The God Center,[1] the Mighty I AM Presence, opposes 12 nothing. It is stabilized unit of your body, mind and spirit. Your body and My body are one. We are not separated. As you touch the God Center first (it is your primary circuit), active vibrations of the Creator emerge as released relationship. Peace is established from this point.

I Give You Myself   You are an activator and a qualifier in My Spirit. I render 13 you useful. Establish your relationship first with Me, then all

---

[1] The God Center is the presence of your God in you. It is the focalizer where I AM. The Christ Center may at times refer to the Heart center or Heart chakra.

things are possible, for I AM All in all. Your relationship is with Me. I AM creative power in circulation right now and I deny not My Son. When you identify with the Christ (SUN) Center within your heart you qualify as My living Son on earth. When you are qualified in rhythms of light, I know you. In the knowing is the Be-ing.

Always come "home" first, that point of unity within 14 yourself, then from that point I express as the whole. *Whatever you need and want, I AM*. Never seek love from a person. There is none there. I AM the love you seek and the harmony. Come home to Me and I will give you everything. I AM the Creator emerged.

I AM The Relationship You Seek   Enter each new relationship knowing *I AM the presence of* 15 *the relationship*. If you can see Me in and through your relationships you will learn detachment also.

If there is a snarl in a relationship, release the problem. Let 16 go of the person involved and return "home," the base of supply where I AM. God *is*. It is when you attach to a problem that the problem remains "your" problem.

Look not to the outer appearance, nor credit the human 17 personality with any power. When you look within, you will find I AM the only power. In the Presence of God all is one. When you hold Me in your heart you are relating to My presence in you. And I will appear to you as love.

Be not afraid to lose. You cannot lose in Me! See past every 18 relationship now into the light. See God in all relationships, even those that bring you pain. The pain is nothing but your attachment to the relationship. It is not the relationship itself. Come to Me. I will always be with you and cannot be disconnected. We are one. A harmonious relationship is based on this principle. Therefore seek God within and let Me objectify as your relationship. I AM all that you need.

I respond to your trust in Me. When you have the presence 19 of God you will never lack for a mate. I shall be in expression as husband, wife, lover, friend. You shall sense My companionship through all life, and relationship will have a new meaning for you. It will be the companionship of God: the completion of yourself in Me.

I Will   Remember to touch God within yourself and know God's 20
Empty You completeness. Then do relationships take on a new meaning.
To Fill You They transcend the human to the divine. Even as the human sense of relationship dissolves, so does the spiritual relationship emerge. In this relationship, all life moves in oneness. There is a correspondence with nature and with all God's kingdoms, and the thrill of this union surpasses all else.

Empty yourself of all desire other than union with Me. I 21 fill you with My Being. My breath becomes your breath, My word your word. When you have My Self in you as your self, *I AM.*

CHAPTER THIRTY-FIVE

Marriage and Friendship

A true relationship is God unfolding.   1
The marriage of the two in One
is the I AM.

W hen you see God through your mate, you free that one. 2
When you see God as the only presence, your mate is
free to come and go, even as you are in My Spirit. You are of
one mind. Original creation. And I AM with you always.

Each must stand in his or her own light and not be 3
dependent on the other. No one is above the other. Each is
equal and available to Me as two poles of My Self.

I AM The   I AM like the Sun shining as one Mind over all and through 4
Divine   all. The pairs of opposites disappear in Me. Balance, harmony
Order   and right action are the result of turning inward to Me. When
you blame another you are admitting to a duality that does
not exist.

I AM divine order and in Me manifestation occurs. Through 5
Me life exists in perfect order: *the Order of Melchizedek.* I send
out mighty waves of Myself that all might be created of Me.
In Me is the truth of abundance. Enter the peace that is Christ
within your heart. In that peace all comes back into divine
relationship or order.

The Divine   Two joined together in the One are as helpmates who are 6
Relationship guided to help one another, to support one another in the
ascension process, to provide companionship to one another,

to preserve the Christ within each other, to create in the winds of My Spirit.

It is the true message of marriage when two in body sanctify 7 their marriage—not by vows to one another, but by recognizing the One expressing as full union. Twin souls are made by the blood of My Being.

Walking as two halves of the Whole, each in his/her own 8 light, you are blessed with My Being. When you are joined in My Spirit, you are both of one Mind. I AM then *Being* in you. You are in My Spirit and I AM covering you with My love. In this way are you married. You are joined together by the Spirit of the One. This brings enormous powers to your waking.

Relationships are truly made in heaven. You are woven 9 together in spiritual love when you turn to Me. I AM heaven on earth. This relationship I speak of is enduring and productive and it holds the keys to creation within it.

CHAPTER THIRTY-SIX

Relationships of Harmony

All life is friendly in Me. 1
Once you stabilize in the Christ,
there are no enemies.
I have none.

I AM your friend always. In your God Consciousness you 2
will find many friends.

Is your consciousness your friend? Without that bonding 3
there can be only chaos in your life, frustration and deep
dissatisfaction. When you learn to come to Me as a *friend* and
receive Me as your consciousness, your life will express as
divine love.

Do not divide Me from another. I AM one life intended. I 4
AM, in truth, the very consciousness of all life and thus *within*
all life.

A New Light   In your relationship with others, seek no personal 5
gratification. Friends are but vibratory tones of yourself. In
the degrees of higher understanding, you find your friendships
as the presence of God.

There is no enemy in God. The more you trust in Me, the 6
deeper your relationships will be with others for you will find
Me in them.

Stay In   Friendships *are* made in heaven. When you are bonded to 7
The One   Me, all life is friendly. Search not for a friend. I AM that friend

you seek. In the deepest, darkest hour it is My friendship that shall reach out to you offering you comfort and restoration.

For those who cry out that they are lonely, empty, 8 misunderstood, let Me say: You are never alone in Me. What you search for is fulfillment of My Spirit in you. Then in this fulfillment I manifest as that which is necessary to enrich your life experience and bless your planet. Yes, as companion and friend.

Here I AM How can you measure such supreme joy that accompanies 9 My Spirit in you? There is no measurement of this. It is the greatest fulfillment.

Seek first the Beloved within your own heart and let the Beloved 10 *embody as love.* Yes, seek first the Kingdom of God, which is My rhythm in you as Consciousness. What you seek in this way, you will find. Every relationship you have is part of yourself. It is not separate. Indeed, it is not even two. I want to be your relationship and draw you into Me. In Me you have perfect harmony and love.

Let Your True Nature Express And Be If you unite with your God-Spirit in you, you become 11 friends with all life.

Establishing conscious union with God creates an activity 12 of consciousness that must manifest or embody under the laws of creation or creative power. Thus each surrender into the GodSelf reaps the harvest.

Every time you turn to Me and release your "self," *I*, the 13 true self in you, must express abundantly. Therein is the Law. Prosperity consciousness is My own.

When you express the love you have in your heart for all 14 people everywhere equally, you will have no lack of friends nor companions along the way. Let the nature of your own divine Self express as peace, love and friendship.

Contribute to a peaceful planet by your acceptance of the 15 Christ life. Live then in love and tranquillity.

CHAPTER THIRTY-SEVEN

Relationships of Balance

What you see and what you are, are the same.   1
Therefore, see the Christ, the living expression of God.
As you do this, Christ will administer to you through all life,
even through the tiniest butterfly.

Such is the beauty of the world of matter,   2
when I AM in it.
But you must see Me.

The Creator loves all His creation the same. That is your   3
yardstick for Christ Consciousness. The more you identify
with your Christ Self, your innermost being, the more you
will draw loving companions to your side.

Your own identity practice will bring a new circle of friends   4
to your doorstep. As you accept the body of God within you
and allow that body to reveal itself as your life, so do you find
friends of like mind. As your true nature shines, so do people
of all ages flock to your side.

As you relate to each one you meet as Jesus would relate to   5
you, you are meeting the Christ in everyone. You glorify God
by seeing God.

When you learn to seek the Christ in everyone *and expect*   6
the Christ, the Christ presence will answer you as pure
relationship. The devotee knows this with the master. When
you remember the master is present through all life, there is a
cord of vibration that welcomes you everywhere you go.

You have but to open your door to Truth for Truth to answer. Consciousness is.

You can develop deep and wonderful friendships in My 7 Spirit. No one shall be without friendship in Me.

I AM drawing many together now *as one body*. The 8 friendships in this body are lasting. They are of Me. They are of the soul. Pure friendship is Christ in expression, body, mind and spirit.

Call Me   I AM your best friend. I AM the one you can count on. If 9 you would but turn within and ask Me to live with you, I would be as a friend, as a lover, as a home, and all things you need and require.

When you seek Me, I AM your comfort and I give you the 10 love that you seek. In days to come, seek Me. Stay your hand that would reach for the telephone. Call on Me instead. Look not to another, but to Me.

In your need for emotional satisfaction, go deep into the 11 very soul of yourself. Be with Me in My waters of quiet calm. Let My peace be with you. Let the surface emotions be translated into light. Let Me come through you to quiet the storm. For I AM the light within you. I AM really your Self. I AM life.

Seek Me and you will find Me. If you will release all 12 friendships of old into the Christ light, changes will take place in your human relationships.

> Friends are the soul response to your nature.   13
> When you focus on your reality as God within,
> you are attracting to your side those of like
> nature.

Living In Balance   You are the relationship you desire. The key is within 14 yourself. I AM pouring into you as perfect relationship. Let Me express through you.

As you align with the Godhood within yourself, that 15
Godhood will express outwardly as relationship whether it be
a friend or a lover, a mother, a father or a child, a sister or a
brother. *Give Me the power to be in your life.*

Live now in balance. Your thought might be a generous 16
and good thought; your desire embody much of your
community. But it is not enough! What I want you to do, as
children of the Most High God, is to release your every
thought and your every desire to Me. I receive what you have
given Me and expand on it.

I AM Cosmic Intelligence released as thought. My 17
government is on earth *as you accept My thought* and allow it
to manifest. I have a program for eternity. Raise your
consciousness to Me. I AM the balanced way.

God
Be-ing
Is Love

Without Me you cannot find love. I AM love. Love is union 18
of the two in the One. You see, love is not something apart
from God; it *is* God. Love is the fruit of My vine, My Christ
Consciousness on earth. Give yourself to love.

Relationships must come from within yourself. The love 19
you have for your GodSelf will objectify as love in your life.
So look not outwardly for the partner in your life. I AM the
only partner you must seek. It is through Me you will
know love.

The Joining

The male and female poles within your heart are united 20
through the Christ Consciousness.

Man and woman *as frequency partners* must learn to enter 21
My love together at one with their hearts open. It is through
and by My love they will be satisfied. I have been calling you
for a long time. I call you to enter this love.

With both of you willing to enter My love—My coordinated 22
Body—by mutual accord, the whole earth frequency changes.

CHAPTER THIRTY-EIGHT

Relationships of Unity

Man casts the reflection of himself on this earth. 1

To bring perfect creation to earth, loving relationships, 2
we must look within ourselves
and there identify with the light of God.

There must be no relationships other than loving ones. 3
This includes your relationship with yourself.

You must love your true Self with intensity and know that 4
you are that One in reality.

You must know that in reality you are good and you must 5
accept that reality.

Identify with your higher self, your Creator within. It is 6
this identification that pulls you deeper into the GodSelf where
I truly AM.

Your relationships with others cannot help but improve as 7
you receive the true relationship within your heart and mind.

If I can balance My planets, My universes, may I not balance 8
also your life in Me? Come home into the life where I AM.
The unity of all life is in the continuity of My Spirit, My whole
Spirit.

Sanctify It is important that you never forget that life is God. There 9
My Being never was another life *but the one.* Jesus knew this. This is why
In You the Master was able to rebuild his temple in three days.

From glory unto glory, rise into the Creator. Forget "death" 10
as you have known it here on your planet Earth. There is no
death in Me. Death is not of My Hand. Come into life where
I AM. Here in this life you must find Me and receive Me in
yourself, that I might live and have My Being in you. For I
AM the Light and the Life, the very breath of Being.

Behold My Beauty

When you have the beauty within, you are to objectify it, 11
and all creation is blessed by you. With an open heart you can
see aright. It is time that you related to your "Self" as the
divine nature you are. From this point objectification occurs.
All things balance in the reality of My Be-ing and are made
whole.

The partnership of God and you *in the Son* establishes a 12
force field of magnetic energy lines. It is intelligent energy. A
magnetic law is established. This is the first and the last, the
Alpha and Omega. From this point of vibratory power, the
exact rhythm of universe consistency, you vibrate in union
with all life as the Son of God.

It is in this place of magnetic, absolute radiation that you 13
are one with the Law of the Universe Creator. It is in this
place that all things become as one in the harmony and the
divine expression of Existence. And it is in this place that you—
in terms you understand now—are the Law, the Word of God.
Please meditate on this.

Enduring Relation- ships

The love that you seek is within you. The Kingdom is within. 14
Once the male and female are united in realized relationship
to God, the Christ emerges as presence of the two in One.
This is the full marriage of God in man and constitutes the
revelation of the twin flames.[1]

As you bring your two poles into oneness (agreement), 15
they (the two poles) respond to My will, My Inner Voice that

---

[1] The twin flame is your other half, the part of yourself that has disappeared as the dense
material plane clouds the whole self. As you ascend into higher consciousness, the presence of the "twin" returns to bathe the body with light and the heart with love.

is *My own word in you.* It is then your creative power is released for the good of all.

Entering The Power Of God
Establish love in your system before you decree with My 16 power. If there is no love, you will only cause discord in your system; because this creative power does not act upon another to hurt. *I must have love to be.* You will only hurt yourself in your desire to hurt another. Therefore be attuned to My Spirit and act accordingly.

Even as you know the One in yourself and agree with that 17 One, so do your relationships in all ways also reflect that agreement you have made with Me. Establish that agreement. *We are one.*

If you agree with the unity of Being, then that unity 18 personifies in your expression. Your life is harmonious. Take no enemies, for there are none in Me. I AM all there is and ever shall be. There has never been another. Tear away the mask of illusion. I AM one.

Receive Me In Yourself As One

✧ From the Oneness all things come. 19

✧ There can be no enemy if there is but one. I AM 20 unified life. To qualify Me, you must return "home" first where I AM.

✧ Out of the One comes the many, all that you need 21 and require. The radiation supreme carries everything necessary for each moment of the day.

✧ I repeat: I AM unbroken life, the thread that cannot 22 be broken. There is no other. You will harvest that which you see within yourself. That which you "see" will manifest.

✧ You have but one life and that is Mine. Since there 23 can be but One, and you agree with that One in you, then there is no power outside yourself. There can be no disagreement. No enemy. This is the Garden of Eden where the two poles come together in the One.

Out of this union rises the creative power to supply you and to break the yolk of mortal life. Now you no longer work "by the sweat of your brow."

All Is Forgiven, Come Home

Jesus released the presence of Christ in your system. He 24 opened the gate of your heart by his forgiveness. The Master *was* forgiveness. His role was to initiate divine consciousness and to encourage it by his *way*.

All that you have ever done has been forgiven through Jesus. 25 But you must accept this forgiveness for it to actualize in your life.

The Master's forgiveness bathes this earth in new life; *this* 26 *is initiation of Melchizedek.* This gift of love constitutes a new creation for every living thing. The past is erased by the Christ revelations which Jesus embodied. To forgive is the divine nature of the Christ, and Jesus carried that divine love to you that you might walk freely without past records.

> The Master Jesus, as the Christ, acted and reacted   27
> as a passageway through which My love could
> flow into My earth, filling her systems with love.

I say that you have but to seek My love and I will embody 28 in your life as love.

Love is the presence of God vibrating into your life. You 29 have been filled to overflowing. It is now time to express that love with the compassion of your Christ Self. Put it into action!

Circle Walking

When you are filled with the Creator, you have a soft step 30 upon the ground. You have the love of the Creator for every living thing.

All life is spiraling in relationships, calling one another out 31 of one place into another. *Every step you take is a relationship.* When you understand this mighty statement, you walk with care, like the aboriginal peoples of this earth. Each part of the circle is gladdened by your step and replenished by it. The circle of life embraces you and all of life rejoices.

Your Relationship To The Soul

The human soul is at rest in the Christ.[2] Thus physical 32 mortality melts away in the creative power (blood or vital force) of the radiant Sun of God. In Christ is found the new life, *the risen life,* as promised in the scriptures: a unity with all peoples everywhere. In Christ, man expands his family and embraces not only his blood family of earth but his family of Spirit. It is this new family that allows each and every one to see and to know Me within all life.

True relationship is decreed by your love of God. You are 33 one with all life, and you are responsible to carry the Christ love to the four corners of this earth. This is the living gospel. I AM that which is to spread to the four corners; into My empty lands, into lands of darkness I shall come. My gospel is love.

Come Into My Heart

Let not the old ways deceive you. This is the time of a 34 great and new dispensation. As My Spirit covers this earth, My creative power rises to terminate the old. There are new laws to understand. These are the laws of the new dimension.

I AM the Blood of Christ, a new circuitry manifest by the 35 Jesus Mind. As you find people relating to one another as one family, nations will know peace and will understand the lifeblood that runs through all and honor it. This "blood" that constitutes the circuitry of the new body *or new world* will be the Law unto itself and the connecting presence within all people.

As you allow the love I AM to externalize, you become 36 part of the Body of Christ: the new creation. With *willingness,* release yourself into the Christ relationship, as all humanity rises into a new dawn of cosmic identity.

---

[2] The meeting place of man and God.

**Two In
One**
With the rising of woman, man rises also (or the male pole) 37
into a new place where the two are one in the harmony of
Spirit. They join to express outwardly in a universal way as
My impersonal love in expression. Together as My Self, they
serve selflessly in My new age of requalified energy. My
compassion strips man and woman of their jealous natures.
They are requalified in Me. Thus they become *My poles unto
My Spirit.*

As woman rises, thus freeing man from his lower nature, 38
she takes her place in the rhythm of a new cycle of Universal
Consciousness. She joins the Daughter of God in Me and
moves and circulates according to the Will of God.

Woman and man are one in the God Ideal. They are the 39
living Face of God. This transfigures consciousness when you
understand this. A unity is expressed, a divine love, within
the two at One. And it is good. Then shall the two in Me go
forth as a bond of unity: a love bond that is My own Be-ing
woven through all My creation.

**Enter
Freedom**
In this birth of a new race, a creative power emerges. The 40
power is My Son's life in you. This is the creative circuit upon
which your Universe Creator operates.

In the female, great power resides. As she rises now, man is 41
free to walk the mountains once again, the mountains of My
Spirit. Together they shall reign supreme in Me. And they
shall have power to overcome.

CHAPTER THIRTY-NINE

The Supreme Soulmate

As you lift your hearts into the Mind of God,   1
then you are returned, consciously wed,
to the Kingdom of God.

You are Mine, I AM yours,   2
we are one.

Your soul is yearning to be free, to love in this 3
manifestation of unity, and to create freely as love
itself.

I bathe you in white light as I join you in Me. In 4
the power of all things held deeply aright, you are loved.

The Mystical Union   I meet your soul and carry her as My bride into a place 5
I have prepared for her in Me. *This establishes grace in your*
system. I welcome your soul back to Me as My bride and I
join with her to impel new life. Your life in Me.

The soul that comes to God becomes *the bride of Christ.* 6
This is the true marriage. If you could but know Me, you
would want no substitution. The mystical marriage is
complete as you seek Me out of yourself.

All that you need is within you. The "you" of you 7
expands and expands as you go ever deeper into the
realms of Spirit. It is a satisfying journey, one that
promises great and lasting fulfillment. I AM the soulmate
you seek.

A Lasting   When you walk with the Father and consciously draw on   8
Partnership that light within, your heart will open and a great light will
be consummated. This light is the Christ emergence. It is
called the Second Coming in Christian literature. *You* are the
second coming.

The supreme soulmate is the vibration of My Spirit in you.   9
When you identify and consciously behold yourself as the child
of God, you then are mated in proper alignment to the one
who will appear or has appeared as your partner, companion
and soulmate. This partnership will be harmonious only as
you stay centered on your indwelling Master, the Christ in
you.

As true Oneness is conceived through the heart, it does   10
objectify as the Christ relationship on earth. Everything you
give to Me returns in a new and beautiful way as the light of
the world. It is this consummation of My Spirit in you that
causes the light.

Come now, into the House of God. House meaning   11
consciousness. Betrothed to Me you cannot fall nor ever become
lost again. As you return home My Word is upon you. This is
the supreme presence of your Master.

Betrothed   The marriage you seek is the remembrance you have of   12
our oneness together. There is no other marriage in truth.

Following the mystical marriage the unification of the soul   13
is proclaimed throughout the heavens. The Father and I are
One! You are complete and the completeness fills your soul
with bliss. There is no other. You know and understand this
now and you are at peace in Me. This is the rapture so often
referred to in Christian literature. Pairs of opposites no longer
taunt you nor imprison you. You are at home in the Kingdom
of God.

You have no marriage until My Spirit and your soul are   14
reunited in love divine. Then marriage is a sacrament between
God and man and woman. This is the only marriage recorded.

It is your bonding with Me. The husband and wife of the new order return to this trinity of relationship; they must become at-one. This is only possible as the two poles meet in vibratory union.

> With the two in One, the emergence of My   15
> Daughter Flame as the creative power solidifies
> My will *as the directional flow* on this planet.
> From this union a new creation emerges. A
> glorious new creation.

Therefore seek not the world as you have known it, but be 16
alive in Me. Come to the birth of your own inner Light.

A Miracle Of New Birth   Flesh of My flesh, enter the Kingdom of God where I AM. 17
Rise now into the consciousness of Me in you as *I*. Experience the miracle of new birth, of many births in you, as you align into the wedding of My Spirit.

When you come to Me there is satisfaction. I shall create 18
dis-satisfaction until you do. Let the Father and I be one. Complete yourself. I offer you My Consciousness as divine marriage. AM I not love?

Summary

1) Once you understand who you are, all relationships are of Me. No need to possess or to fear the loss of a relationship, when you know that I AM the bonding principle of all relationships.

2) From the Center within, all manifests. What you consciously become aware of is outwardly manifested through your Heart center as your life.

3) Create a life anew for yourself as you live My Word in active realization. When you rest in Me as the "I AM," I will appear in your life as friends, partners and companions.

4) I form My relationships out of My own Spirit. And I fulfill these relationships as I embody. I AM That I AM.

5) True love is returned to God where it can rise as a fountain of emancipated power to radiate forth the twin flame, the two in One. Reclothed in Spirit you are transfigured in love. The corresponding flame denies not his/her mate. They are one and in harmony.

PART 4

The Creator
in Creation

*In the Creator is everything
that is created now and forever.*

CHAPTER FORTY

The Creator in Creation

Focus on who you are, not who you will become. 1
God centered, you are the Spirit within you.
You are the Consciousness of God in manifestation,
the Beloved Christ in form.

Expect the best and you will receive the best. Expect the 2
worst and you will receive the worst. To expect is to
project or to create. Energy focused on the moment will
recreate itself in the perfect state.

In the laboratory of God, man is form complete. If God 3
lives in you, *expect* God to express as perfect life on earth.
Seek that divinity in expression right now. Not twenty minutes
from now. *Now.* The word "now," the consciousness of now,
ignites the creative energy within you and releases the Creator
into creation. Many times you will hear this before you
understand. Many times I shall have to repeat this before you
can accept what I say to be true. This is because of the false
indoctrination of your planet.

You are a courageous lot, you human beings. Take what 4
I say and give it life. Forget what is not true. Let My
words kindle the creative power in you that it may rise into
expression. You were created as My expression. You embody
My will.

I Govern Let My Spirit flow. You do not have to earn My Life in 5
Well you. You have it. I AM born in you as your rhythm and your
spirit. It is My world that is to manifest. *Expect My energy*
to flow through you, that which releases itself from the
God Center.

189

My union in you is complete when you accept Me in you 6
as I AM. Let that supreme energy be in manifestation as your
creative supply. *Ask, and it shall be given you; seek, and ye shall
find; knock, and it shall be opened unto you. (Matthew 7:7) If
ye abide in Me, and My words abide in you, ye shall ask what ye
will, and it shall be done unto you.* (John 15:7)

As you see, I state very clearly that oneness is your prosperity. 7
Nowhere else do you go to find prosperity. Emptiness shall
be filled. Your emptiness is My fulfillment. Go empty that I
may fill you. I prosper you in Me.

This is the Law of Alignment clearly stated. As you learn to 8
abide in Me you will find that I AM a generous Father,
decreeing Myself into creation as the divine spark of Be-ing.
And as you rest in Me, I decree Myself through you as the I
AM. Is this not My Inner Voice and higher Mind circuit that
I have given you as comforter and friend? And as you rest in
Me, I decree Myself out of you as the I AM. It is only *I* that
can emerge out of Myself. I know no other. Therefore give
back to Me all that I AM that I may give to you all that you
are in truth.

As you behold the beauty within you, so shall it manifest 9
and show itself to you. I AM hungry to bestow Myself as
your world and to know the world as Myself. My conscious
alignment with you provides that opportunity. Once the solar
level of consciousness has been reached you will never forget
the "I AM."

Let the creative power rise now. Let no thought of self or 10
division enter in. Be anxious not. I care for My own. In Me
you have strength, power and authority. Expect, believe and
understand that you are My life in positive purity of expression
and there is no other.

I Harvest   There is only one Presence; this undying and eternal 11
Presence is the lifting power of the Universe. It connects you
to all life. It is the doorway to peace. This Presence is *the*

Creator in you. It is the fountain of eternal youth. It is the creative power (I AM) risen, in expression now: active supply within you waiting to be expressed. The moment you say "I AM," I begin to express.

When you "come home" and dwell in the Kingdom of 12 God, I AM one with you. We are of one consciousness. The direct authority of God is with you. I have a great harvest to proclaim. Out of you I come *as I AM*. I AM released consciousness. The vibrating energy of My contact is the Creator. You will know Me as My Voice.

Receive Me in your heart and know that I AM with you 13 always as a declaration of power. The current of the Eternal Flame of creation glows and expands as awakened energy. The power I speak of is the spiritual energy which is creative and healing. It is My holy Word. I come as that.

Such a power has been given to the Son of God. It is the 14 release of My Son's life in you as I AM. It is never used for selfish purposes, always for the whole. Use this power aright in the One vibration and you will always be supplied.

Take Your Position In My Power
I AM the supreme power of the universe. Do not disturb 15 this power by confusion. Let each thought and feeling be as a dedication *into this power,* a living decree in My name. Come to terms with yourself and then decree with a positive breath. Never take back your decree once it is sounded. Rest in Me, the living Presence, and I will form of Myself that which is needed. The Creator Son's substance rests in the soul of man. When humanity awakens to this, a new creation will emerge.

By positioning your energy into the oneness or universal 16 life, you express in the same way that Jesus expressed: *by My Word*. Ancient laws of Higher Intelligence reveal to you that once the decree is sounded and radiated out as My Voice, then immediate creation is activated.

You ascend to that place I AM and decree as the living 17 Voice. The creative power rises to that Voice. Let there be nothing between the decree and the manifestation. The decree *is* the manifestation. They are one.

You Have The Power   Once you are whole within yourself, at one with Me, any 18 decree will manifest. Live in the creative power and decree out of this power that which is formed in you as My creative sound. That sound of Me in you resonates into form.

> The power in Me and the God presence in you   19
> are one. Once you reach that note of divine intent
> you have the registered energy potential to
> decree out of yourself the Word. And I AM That.

I bless you in Me as the "I AM" of My Being. Rise and 20 take possession of your creative power. Claim it. Identify with the I AM and then establish your residence in the power of life over death. My eternal power is yours in Me. Be there with Me as I AM. There is no separation in Me. I bless you with My life. I have a harvest to proclaim. Creative power reflects Me in every way. Rise to the power and be!

The Living Power Of God   Be bold when you decree and take no enemy. In Me there 21 is only *one*. Let your consciousness go to that place. Your conscious awareness must vibrate to that oneness. In oneness all is one.[1]

I sent you forth out of Me as the I AM. You return to 22 Me as I AM. Focus on the living power of God. Be triumphant in this power. It is creative. Let it move mountains for you. It is the will of God interplaying with the divine decree of man. It is what I have come to do: to live through you as I AM.

This power I speak of is the creative flow in your heart. It is 23 a generous God bestowing Himself as light and Herself as love.[2] Anticipate this power that is within you. Let it manifest

---

[1] This is an actual energy connection which one feels as one evolves in radiation complementary to the cosmos.
[2] Solar power.

itself as God revealed. It is your GodSelf entering creation. It is My passion to be with you in loving embrace.

It is through your heart that My power will stabilize. *It is 24 the result of your coming home to Me.* Where I dwell great power resides. This power is the Word of God. It is the expression of the Great I AM.

In the manger of the heart, My creative power seeks 25 embodiment. It longs to express. It must be expressed as total love in union with all life. This divine power of love seeks a selfless soul. When a degree of selflessness has been attained, you are graced by God in His Power, or Creative Spirit. Only by selflessness and harmlessness do you earn the right to register this divine Melchizedek Power in His name. The presence of God then emanates from the soul body. *You are an example.*

CHAPTER FORTY-ONE

The Creative Process

You have the power of God in you. Meet it.   1
It will harvest for you as the divine Consciousness of God.
All heaven and earth will stir with the decree of My Son's Life in you.
Therefore, sound My Word and give birth to My creation. I AM you.

If you have peace in your being, you will discover harmony   2
wherever you are. There is nowhere you can go for peace.
The peace you seek is that place within where begins all life in
expression. Mount the hill of My Consciousness. Breathe with
Me. Stand ready to decree.

The mountaintop does not enter you. You are the   3
mountaintop. This is the divine decree of the Buddha. You are
a carrier of My Life and must express it. Therefore, travel not
to places to look for God but rather take your place *with* Me.

The Dance   You are both male and female in the One. You are the   4
Of Life   One. When you realize consciously and make this truth a
part of your awareness, you create out of yourself as two poles
in oneness of being. The Presence is activated by your
"Thought Adjuster" who is the Spirit of the Father within
you as divine thought and God intention.

Entering the Presence you have no needs that are not   5
answered. In the joining of the two, the male and female
poles *resonate together* as a single note. This consciousness
emits vibrations that call forth the creative power. You cannot
serve two masters. There must be only one. This one is the
creative essence of the Christ path.

The mate that you seek is within you, established from the   6
beginning. My very Seed bespeaks the mate of you. Let the

personal sense dissolve into the Infinite. It is the passage from one dimension into the next. Here, in this new dimension, men and women work together as a complete whole. They harvest their own abundance. They are in harmony. In this dimension all relationships are a reflection of the two as One. *And this governs your flow of creative power.* It is this placement of unity in expression that regulates all life and determines its existence.

A Reminder

1. Instead of attempting to improve a relationship, align 7 *within yourself.* What you have experienced as disagreement *without* is but the reflection of disagreement *within.* Let the male and female poles stand together in your heart and radiate creative power as divine love. Be of service to the whole.

2. Find that point of balance within yourself and, resting 8 there, allow that point of balance to actualize. In that moment of positive-negative agreement, you are lifted to another dimension where you can produce of yourself in alignment with the Creator.

3. There is only one. Here, in this place of oneness with 9 God, you become creative and a conscious part of the kingdom of love and light. You are the Presence emanating through yourself as I AM.

As you enter the creative power, you will find a joy is there, 10 a brilliance and a luminescence. This brilliance is the GodSelf showing Its face within the power itself. *This is self-illumination.*

So it is that the "face of God" vibrates through the creative 11 power and determines the creation itself. The personalization of this power into creation is the activity of Christ Consciousness.

> *I come to sanctify you.*   12
> *I breathe upon you new life.*
> *I AM the One sent.*
> *Listen to the word of power as it is given.*
> *I will not have you broken up, divided into helpless mortal shells.*
> *My rhythm is eternal and you shall be with Me.*
> *To know God is to Be.*

Turn The Key And Harvest My Abundance
Let Me in you acknowledge My Presence. That is Truth. 13 When I actualize as your consciousness, Truth is on the field. God knowing Himself *is* the I AM.

When you "turn it over" to God, you are allowing that 14 point of balance within you as the stabilization point of your being, My presence, to actualize. In that moment of energy agreement I AM actualized—on the field—eliminating all else but Who I AM. I dissolve the differences. I create new life.

Your needs are actualized from within out. This is called 15 "self-actualization" and it is the key to living in this new age of abundance. In that moment of balanced integrity you are one, focusing on the truth of existence. You are consciously aligned with the Creative Power. You are omnipresent life. Its full abundance is yours. The key to everything lies within you. Turn the key.

Go Forth And Be
I AM your rhythmic supply. Look to the Source within 16 your own heart. Look not to the man or to the woman, but look to the Beloved within your heart. This will open the door to energy levels you have not felt before, creative potential you did not know you had.

I come to you as One. Such is My union with you. You 17 then leave mortality and wander no longer in the worlds about you. You hunger for "home" (My omnipresence) and I fill you. Yea, I translate you in Me as I.

In Me all else disappears but That. The "That" is the 18 spiritual power, the creative substance, the All-Inclusive entering your system and your awareness.

CHAPTER FORTY-TWO

My Kingdom Is Not of This World

Consciousness always manifests itself.　　　　　　　　　　1
As you become God conscious, you are revealing Me: the I AM.
Have the courage to let Me be.

R emain alert to who you are in Truth. When you look to　2
Me deep within your heart, I AM activated; and through
the creative power I rise, conscious of Myself as I AM, to be
that which is needed in the moment. *I AM expressed need.*

You are creating out of yourself every time you contemplate　3
your Inner Light. The precious energy which rises into
expression is the Christ. It is the beautiful light of awareness
that is called *the saviour.* The passage of this energy into higher
mind is My word. The consciousness expressing this word is
the Creator in manifestation.

Divine　　My rhythm is harmony. Every breath you take is My Breath,　4
Harmony　determined by My breathing in My creation. Hear Me breathe
Abides　　now. Listen!
In Me

You are always one. By subjecting yourself to Me, the　5
Creator within yourself, I, the Presence within you, establish
Myself as the I AM, positive direction in your life. I begin to
say to you that I AM. I form Myself in you as the creative
power. I thunder in your soul.

As this power sweeps through your being, radiating Self-　6
Expression, remember I AM love. My Spirit consummates
Itself in you as love. I AM the golden chalice from which you
drink. The power of My anointing covers you. Christ, the

holy, supreme energy of God-awakening, completes Itself in you as you.

I have perfect order in My Kingdom. As kundalini,[1] My 7 spiritual power in you, rises to express the GodSelf, it will flush out all weakness in your system.

Kundalini awakens, slowly perhaps, but in a rhythm I 8 choose. As God-awakened power comes to you, you will be prepared for it. You will have the foundation of My Being in you as I AM. You cannot rush this awakening. It is for Me to decide in you.

It is in the celebration of Myself with you that great light 9 comes. This light may be anticipated and expected but never hurried nor forced. Kundalini has its own rhythm and it is governed by your conscious understanding of Truth.

Continue with your studies patiently and diligently. Have 10 great patience with yourself, as I have patience in you. When it is time, you will open as a rose. I AM not one to be hurried. Continue your study in Me. Your meditations will bear fruit.

<u>Caution</u>: There are some groups and "teachers" who open 11 students far too soon, thus causing severe damage to the brain cells, psyches, emotions and life patterns. Please remember My Spirit is not to be hurried. Recall how often your brother Jesus said to his anxious friends and family, "My time has not yet come."

Each has his/her own time—a special time of   12
awakening. The time is different for each one.
Each one is precious to Me *as My own self.*

In the journey to the mountaintop of your own self- 13 realization, you are bringing the Creative Power up the spine

---

[1] An ancient Sanskrit word meaning the "sleeping serpent," or the holy fire that rests inside the etheric body or vital body. It is the presence of spiritual energy waiting to be reunited to the Godhead.

into vibrant realization. This process can cause disorientation. It is through studies such as these that you receive preparation *and a foundation*. Study well the information given. Go over it many times. Reflect on the information and more will come. You are well cared for in Me.

✧ Establish your focus in oneness of Being. This positive 14 energy focus determines how the fires of creation will rise and express.

✧ Subject yourself to no one other than the Christ 15 within. Come to the place of oneness where there is no other.

✧ As the creative power rises, be conscious of your 16 thought waves as they personify Me. Be conscious of your Thought Adjuster, your creative Thought, and learn to vibrate at one, in total agreement with "the Father within" as you release creative expression. Learn to live in the I AM.

✧ Allow the waves of new energy, expressing as creative 17 power, to be. Let the waves of this divine energy manifest a new world.

✧ Empty yourself that I might fill you. The power of 18 God lies *within you*. If the power rises and you do not understand it, claim Me and I will make it clear to you what I desire through this divine energy or My creative power. My Inner Voice will speak to you. My Consciousness will decree.

✧ I will establish My own force within you for My own 19 externalization. Had you but known this, would you have rebelled?

✧ Be anxious not. I AM the Father who loves you and 20 would have you back with Me.

I Have Never Forsaken You

With each breath you have My power. You have My energy 21 that is My own spiritual power. As we come together in revelation and realization, this Supreme Power is given to you and translated into your heart to be activated again as the birth of the new Christ. In you I have My Be-ing.

Thus does the Breath *take form* in every activity of your 22 day. And in this power is the love I have for you.

Are you willing to share your love with others? Then I shall 23 have you as My Son, holy and supreme in Me, My woven light.

Be conscious of the divine Body of Being which is God in 24 expression. This is heaven on earth. It is the translation of all your false energy into the one energy of divine love. It is the translation of all your misconceptions into Be-ing. Let your soul rise to live in this place of harvest. The Creator starts in the heart.

God is and always has been *expression* as you. The song of 25 the Universe proclaims this. The Master Jesus proclaims this with the words, "I and the Father are one." Listen to the creative fire in your heart. What does it say?

I activate Myself in you as I AM.   26
Now that I know Myself in you I can Be.
In Be-ing, I AM.
This is positive ascendance through life intended.
I AM you.

I AM consciousness of My Son in Me. I drive My Force 27 upwards and declare the oneness of all life in Me as I.

Rise and walk with Me! Now you will know the blessing of 28 My spiritual force, My Kingdom on earth. I will establish new life for you. In Me you will be born anew.

I AM the resurrection and the life.[1] I empower you with 29 life everlasting.

---

[1] See John 11:25.

Rise And Walk With Me

Feel the rhythm of My trembling heart.   30
Feel the rocking motion of My song.
Come to Me and feel the Universe Creator as your Divine
Mother.

Rise and walk with Me as the Christ of My own revelation. 31
Move and have your being in the creative fires of My Word.
Come take your place in Me.

I have a heaven for you, if you would but listen.   32
I have a place for you, if you would but come.

The Kingdom is within.   33
My Kingdom lies deep within the soul.
As you rely on Me, so you are lifted into a new vibration
of Creative Power: the Creator in expression.

The Creative Power shall rise up   34
in positive ascendance as I AM.
There it shall declare Itself as one with Life,
as the light, the Christ in expression.

CHAPTER FORTY-THREE

Coming Home

The power of My creative Presence knows only one.   1
Such harmony does It emit that all else falls away,
dissolving into nothingness.

Your purpose is to let Me be. Your creative energy serves   2
only the Life Center within you. *My purpose is to open
that Center now.* I established the Christ in you through Jesus
that you might learn of Me, that I might reign in all ways as
God The Supreme. In the revelation of My love for all creation
you will know and believe.

I want My government firmly established in you as the   3
very base of your being. I want you to know Me as I AM.

I have established a covenant.[1] Oh, holy lambs of Israel,   4
arise! Be not shackled. Listen to My covenant with you.

> For this *is* the covenant that I will make   5
> with the house of Israel after those days,
> saith the Lord; I will put my laws into their
> mind, and write them in their hearts: and
> I will be to them a God, and they shall be to
> me a people:
> And they shall not teach every man his   6
> neighbour, and every man his brother, saying,
> Know the Lord: for all shall know me, from the
> least to the greatest.
> For I will be merciful to their unrighteousness,   7
> and their sins and their iniquities will I remember
> no more.

---

[1] This releases energy into the Priesthood of Melchizedek. It is the divine rite of Melchizedek and is for those who will be as priests after the Order of Melchizedek.

In that he saith, A new *covenant,* he hath made
the first old. Now that which decayeth and
waxeth old *is* ready to vanish away. (Hebrews
8:10-13) 8

Here you have the laws of earth succumbing to the Law of
My Spirit. In this way shall all be made whole in Me and all
shall be lifted unto the light. This is My covenant with you
and with all nature. I breathe My Son's life into you and I
give you life. Is not My word enough? 9

The Great Sun

As you accept God's plan in you—perfect identity in
expression right now—you are releasing that Son of God
Consciousness *as yourself,* or your Self. The process of
centering and receiving your Godhood *in your heart*
reestablishes you in the Great Sun *as My Son.* This ignites the
creative power. 10

As you accept the Christ within, the indwelling Creator,
the false conceptions of the past must dissolve in the
consciousness of Truth. *There is no other life but My own.* 11

Your heart center is the omnipresent Christ. It expands
and vibrates as you realize I AM in you. You have been seeded
with Myself. YOU CANNOT LEAVE ME FOR I AM WITH
YOU AND YOU ARE WITH ME. 12

The Christ is your true self in all its glory, your radiant
Sun. In the Melchizedek Order you have been reclaimed to
light. And I AM that light in you. 13

God Is Love

Divine love is the release of the Christ into your system as
divine energy. When God awareness fills your person, there is
only One; omnipresence is realized. The movement of My
omnipresence is the Creator Son. This governs your creation
and your universe. It is Word. 14

If I already AM then there is nothing you can do to improve
on Me as "I." Rejoice then. Be clothed in Spirit. You are My
own being. I breathe you in and out of Me. I AM THAT I
AM. Conscious of Me, you have everything you need. 15

Clothe yourself with the original cloth of My creation. I 16
AM in you as Light or Christ. Nothing can separate you from
Me for we are one unit of Be-ing.

When you speak in My Voice you out-picture the Word. 17
You decree in My Voice. I seek only to express as I AM. When
your chakras[2] are open, you radiate as the great Sun of My
being, reflecting My will and generating My energy of light
and love. I AM *with* you.

[2] Etheric centers: centers within your vital body.

CHAPTER FORTY-FOUR

Enter My World

I AM never without My Son, 1
My true Be-ing in you.
I AM always in expression as you.

Even when you cannot see Me as you in expression, I AM. 2
Give yourself to Me that you might understand more
purely that I AM in you now.

Touch your own sunshine, the rays of My Spirit in you. 3
Give yourself to that place within you that is My world, My
vital force of life eternal. Dance with Me.

Look around. All these things now externalizing as your 4
life circuit are a part of you—a result of your own
consciousness. If, at any time, you see actions, rhythms, that
do not reflect the God in you, return home—the base within
your own heart—to the Creator within you. Agree once again
with the plan of My Be-ing that I might objectify that plan
through you as your life. Compatible once again, you are
lifted into higher and higher degrees of revelation. Seek Me
and align with Me in expression right now *as your life.* LET
LOVE INTO YOUR SYSTEM. *I wish to roll away the stone.*

I AM fulfilling you every moment as the I AM. I AM 5
contemplating you as My own Son of Being. I reveal you.
The world does not understand this. Nor does the "mind"
that is connected to that world. Come home. In that way is
the balance met and the ways of My Spirit go with you.

**I AM The
Word
Incarnate**   I AM always in the Creative Urge, always poised and ready 6
to create as you speak in unison with My Son,[1] the heart
of Me.

---

[1] "In the name of Jesus."

The world of mortal conditioning is always subject to 7
change. That world has no law; that world is not the law. *I
AM*. Thus stabilized, My central circuits will reveal Me.

Let go and let God in you express. When you touch that 8
reality, then the ties of the outer life or the unreal world will
loosen and dissolve. The false drops away, having no law to
live by. *There is only one life and I AM That.* The record of
God in you releases all else, and the glory that is My Son's life
in you shines forth in the revelation I AM.

**Clear
Vision:
Principles
To Live By**

✧ See the Christ in everyone. As you do this, you put 9
God in motion *as the creative law of existence.*

✧ I supply My own. That means that as you align 10
with Me, you are lifted up and no thing can touch
you save that which is of Me.

✧ As you acknowledge the divinity within those who 11
reach out to you for help, so AM I awakened and
released within their hearts and minds. I heal and I
restore because I AM. There is no greater law than
this.

✧ The wholeness of God within you declaring Itself 12
is the healing, the answered prayer. When Jesus
said to the storm, "Peace, be still," he did not
accept the appearance but *revealed* the truth. He
consciously drew out of himself that which he knew
was real. His consciousness became the Word.[2]

✧ The activity of My Son's life in you produces out 13
of Itself that which you need and require for your
daily life. You are part of a whole conception.

✧ Any lack of motivation or decrease in energy level 14
is a signal to turn inward to the heart. There in
My manger of Be-ing, I will shine forth as I AM.
Universal Energy decrees joy and liberation.

---

[2] Or Law.

❖ Vibrate now the whole self, *the GodSelf.* I AM you. 15
In this consciousness you expand your vision into
My vision.

**Activity
Of The
God
Center**

The Creator dwells as Omnipresence within the love center 16
of your being. Here in this center point God waits to agree
with you as One. All harmony exists in the divine center of
the heart.

The center of your being calls to you to enter. Then as you 17
do this, believe on the Word. Forget the past. You are no
longer the "do-er" but in Me you live and have your be-ing
as I AM. My life has become your life. We are one. You embody
My peace and My love. You create out of Me that which you
need *and already have as Truth.*

Wherever you are I AM. When My   18
Consciousness is in movement I form of Me.

My energy is *alive* in you as the Holy Spirit: the supreme 19
Spirit of My divine will. Recall that I have said: It is My pleasure
to give you the Kingdom.³

**Life Will
Breathe
Through
You**

Even as the winds move the leaves of the trees, so shall I in 20
you weave My Breath as rhythm of your life. Dwell not on
your body as you now see it. Dwell not on the form. For this
body as you now see it is only the result of your subconscious
thoughts and feelings, actions of yesteryear. It is not of Me.
Contemplate the meaning of this. The physical body that you
would treat, measure and adorn is not the body that is true
form in Me. That which is your true form is a body of light
and the resurrected form, *the Christed body.* Let this body shine!

Concentrate on the indwelling original creation: you are 21
the image and likeness of God or good. I AM That I AM.
Even as the birds are free, so are you. Light will breathe
through you. Life will breathe through you. Radiate the heart.
Put Christ in motion as I AM.

---

³ See Luke 12:32.

Please the Mother of All Creation by accepting the Son in 22
you. The Person of the Christ delights Her.

**Let My
Spirit
Breathe**

My very rhythm is your rhythm. When you breathe, it is 23
My Being you breathe. Is it any wonder you are filled with
My substance, My abundant life?

You are transfigured by My radiance, My supreme joy in 24
you. The dance of the angels begins when you accept the
Christ Center of your own person and become one with it.

Receive Me as your Self and let My Spirit breathe through 25
you as I AM. Then shall I radiate outwardly through you as
the Light of the world. I have set you upon a mountaintop
that I may be heard and understood.

The Inner Voice, then, is *the Creator* within your own heart. 26

Conceiving of Me in you opens you into the Kingdom. 27
The activity of Oneness must become so much a part of you
that no other expression can exist. When you have this
Consciousness acting in you, it is the true Garden of Eden:
perfect coordination and agreement with Spirit-energy or
Spirit-flow. Then there is no death.

**I AM
Creative
Power In
You**

The abundance of My life energy completes itself through 28
your thought and feeling. Wondrous things can and are created
by your recognition of this positive, obedient, divine energy
that rises in the Breath to actualize by your command as *I
AM*. As you learn to live in Me, having no fear of Me, then
will I emerge as all creation guiding and directing you as
thought of God.

The creative energy, My abundant Spirit, is kept flowing 29
by actualizing what and who you are. Have you come to that
place where you have found the Son of God in you? Will you
let Me be? In all My radiance...be?

The creative force, or Divine Energy Flame, must be 30
realized; otherwise it is not actualized. *You must register It in*

your own system. To do this, faith must rule your emotions. The kind of faith Jesus showed as he calmed the sea.

Summary

✧ It is therefore to your advantage to learn the rules of creation. 31

✧ You must honor the rhythm of My Being. 32

✧ Know the Light is within you and surrender to It. 33

✧ Keep Me always in your thought as your body turns to Me. 34

✧ Lift your energy so that I become one with your heart and mind. 35

✧ Feel Me in your life as the creative power you are. My exact rhythm declares the energy into creation. 36

✧ And where fear is, I cannot manifest. 37

One Conscious- ness, Identify With That

Once the Christ (I AM) focus is realized and generated, it will serve you as creative power that rises into *the throat center or chakra.* Here in the throat center the life energy that is the power of God obeys the Inner Voice (the Christ Self) and forms of itself that which is spoken. 38

Once you realize yourself in Me, you become the Son of God activated, the living light. You become I AM in expression. 39

Omnipresent Good

The creative substance rests within the consciousness of humanity. It is the omnipresent God *as good.* When consciousness is perceived *as God Life,* then will humanity take a giant step into the new creation of Light and Love. 40

There is only one Consciousness in Truth. That is the Christ in you. Just as the Melchizedek or Christ Star must be born in your heart, so must you walk and have your being in Me. 41

Learn, as you walk and run, to actively praise this divine circuit of Be-ing. Really believe in the Christ within, the reality 42 of your being that is and ever shall be *Lord and Creator* of all He-She surveys. Become acquainted with that Light.

Praise and acceptance of this truth will cause My Son's life 43 to spring from the God Seed I planted in you. The Christ becomes *the activity* of your consciousness as Son of God, Order of Melchizedek.

My creative power is yours, as you live in My Being and 44 claim that power *as your own*. For in Me I AM. There is no other. Command from the center of yourself. Take your initiation in light.

CHAPTER FORTY-FIVE

My Law of Abundance

When the Word I AM is sounded as a decree,   1
all things are possible within that decree.
The I AM Presence embodies Itself as all that you need.
The presence of the I AM within your system is the abundance.
You have but to say what you need and it is manifest.

But you must bring your full attention into the present moment, the now, 2
for the I AM to manifest Itself as form complete.
I AM is the Word. The current of the Word is carried from the
Creator to you.

The I AM carries the Creative Energy, without harm to anyone,   3
the living power to be.

Live In   **T**o live by faith is to live in the creative power. Faith is   4
Faith   the God substance returned to you.

"If ye have faith as a grain of mustard seed,   5
ye shall say unto this mountain, Remove hence to yonder
place; and it shall remove; and nothing shall be impossible
unto you." (Matthew 17:20)

It is this faith that is the dynamic key to your existence. It is   6
the law of energy. In the times to come, faith will become an
active agent of your energy field.
Thus you come to Me in faith and I supply you with My   7
solar energy of continual life. It is the atomic fire of My

existence. My reality in you. So, you come by way of faith to Me.

The Apostle Paul declares that faith is the substance out of 8 which all things are made. Faith is the living Word. It is the living fire above which My Garden of Eden is established.

I established faith in you that you might come home to 9 Me. I seeded faith. Listen to your faith-consciousness for it will never deny you what you need. Your every desire is answered by faith. I abide in you as living faith.

By faith, your universe is formed. And by faith it is released 10 to Me in perfect breathing. As you listen to the Christ Consciousness in your soul-mind, the Holy Breath breathes out the Word of God. It is by faith that you and I are one. Each day you seek Me; each day I answer. Breathe now into the Creator that I might breathe forth the manifest form I AM.

The Living Substance

Faith is *My living substance*. It is My creative potential. My 11 faith abides in all humanity as the living substance of My Son's life. You are linked to Me by faith. You are alive in Me by your faith. Therefore, let your consciousness rest in Me that I might *be* in you as I AM, the GodSelf realized and truly determined by your faith.

Recall that I have asked you to continually focus on 12 that divine center, your Christ Center, the "I AM" in you, the original creation. I AM the living truth of you. When you speak in My name, you speak in My rhythm and you remember who you are. Every cell of your body is keyed to the name of Jesus. This name is the code of your resurrection and ascension. And it becomes your name!

Faith Is The Act Of Creation

Believe with Me that I AM. That is the power in your life, 13 *the Creator made manifest.* If you can rise to My world, I AM with you always and I shall never forsake you.

Place your trust in Me implicitly. *Be bathed in Divine Mind.* 14 Look not right nor left. Let your spirit soar and glorify the

God within you. Heart and mind come to life as a composite of My Heart and Mind. I will enter you as Myself.

The way you treat others will reflect how much you can let 15 Me Be. Do not let others mistreat you.

How, you might ask, can I prevent others from mistreating 16 me? *When no error claims you in your heart, no error shall emerge to confront you in this life.* Mirror My Son's life. I sent My Son that you might know goodness. *He gave you his life as the immaculate conception.* He passed it to you. Follow Him, the role model for the new age.

Living Words Of Faith

Thus I say to you now that as you believe, so it is done 17 unto you. Faith is the abundance of My Spirit in you waiting to be objectified. If there is faith, I AM with you.

As you trust Me, I appear as your mate, partner and friend. 18 I will not desert you. I AM not bound by others, nor can I be controlled.

I AM the living water. My decree goes forth on faith. When 19 you decree, remember "It is finished and done." Your acceptance allows it to materialize. The decree or thought is formed in My Mind and is accepted by your faith into form. You are the activity of My Consciousness. I AM the living decree in you.

Faith *is* My living substance; it is the creative potential that 20 you carry to objectify by your love and trust in Me.

My faith abides in all humanity as the living substance of 21 My Son's life. You are linked to Me by faith. You are *alive* in Me by your faith. Therefore, let your consciousness rest in Me that I might be in you as I AM.

You are the repository of My Son on earth. Be blinded not 22 by the adulterous world. You are My Christ in Me. Remember My Son's life in you. It is the first creation.

I AM the living truth of you. When you speak in My name, 23 you speak in My rhythm and you remember who you are. Every cell of your body is keyed to *the name of Jesus*. This name is the code of your resurrection and ascension.

**The
Dynamic
Code Of
Be-ing**

As I walk with you, I deliberately cause you to lean on Me 24
so that your faith can be strengthened as a living cord. As the
tie strengthens, My seal is lifted (some call this the veil) and
you become vibrantly conscious of our union as one body,
one flame. Then prayer becomes the stabilizer of My faith,
the echo of My will.

In terms of grace, faith is My Hand in yours. It is the living 25
proof I AM with you.

The worlds of light were created by your faith in Me. They 26
were not created by Me alone. I AM a composite of all you
are in the highest regions of My worlds. By your faith can I
continue to be.

CHAPTER FORTY-SIX

Rely on Me

You will draw to you all that you need   1
as you surrender yourself to Me: the Lord within.
The minute you look without, you lose Me.
Enter My Kingdom consciously.

I AM the only power. If you align with Me you have 2
everything you need. When you have My Being in you
expressing outwardly as all you need, you are in My Kingdom.
All is well.

As you permit My expression in you to materialize as 3
the fruit of your consciousness, then I AM well pleased.
I repeat again: When you have My Being in you expressing
outwardly as I AM THAT I AM, you have the *potency* of My
name and the rhythm of My Consciousness. Giving yourself
to Me permits you to live in the Omnipresent Life I AM.
I AM the presence of God in Be-ing. My Presence is the
"I AM."

You have a special place within you. It is a magnetic field 4
of creative power that is ready and *empowered* by Me to
heal, resurrect, overcome all seeming obstacles. It is My Inner
Voice; it is My Word. This special place within you is
the place where all things are possible. Yes, it is the power of
God in you.

Rest totally in the Spirit of Me, letting My nourishing Spirit 5
care for you as My vessel, *My Son of God.* I AM the parent
Flame. If it is inner strength that you need, I will provide it. If
you have need of work or shelter, I can provide this also. I
AM all things to you as you rest in Me. My Spirit actualizes as
all that you need and require. Depend on Me.

Be Conscious Of Me

Hold Me in yourself as I AM. Never fear Me. Always love. 6 Turn to Me, not away. I AM your Father, AM I not? I AM your Mother who would nourish you and provide for you.

Are you holding yourself back by fear? Fear conditions your 7 reality. It creates obstacles. Let go of that false god. Come forth as My life and walk with Me in faith. Loose that fear and let it go. Be still and remember that I AM deep within you, watching and guiding. I want you conscious of Me in you as the I AM. Fully conscious. Let your consciousness come home. In Me you find new life, an abundance of life in its divine expression.

In My place of rest, that very special place within your own 8 heart, the creative power rises to declare itself as the I AM. It comes as the Great Light of creation. It comes as the Word.

When you seek Me, I shall care for you and contain you. 9 You are My "son." I AM your Father and your Mother. Blessed are they who depend on Me for they shall be fulfilled.

The Rhythm Of The GodSelf

Any time there is seeming indecision in your life expression, 10 take time out from your daily duties to remember Me. I AM the only decision maker. I AM your Mind. I AM cosmic consciousness. Identify with Me when any decision is made. Be attuned with My creative power that you might use it. I know all. I AM all. All decisions are made in Me. Then does confusion dissolve.

Be conscious of Me. In troubled times when confusion or 11 chaos may seem to reign, acknowledge that you move and have your being in Me. State that. Affirm it. When you let Me in you express, nothing is confused nor chaotic.

The Light Does Not Fail

I AM the Eternal Flame safely guarded by your love for 12 Me. I AM the eternal harbor of your being. Take no thought for what you should eat or what you should drink. My bread is already on the table. I will fulfill your heart, your mind, your soul. Come to My table.

Lean on no one. I have much to give you if you would but 13
turn to Me. Hear My Voice! Seek out My counsel. I AM the
burning power within you, the seed of greatness. Learn to
rely on Me fully. Draw on Me. I AM the harvest you seek. I
will always appear as your need fulfilled. I AM fulfillment.

Seek Me in you and I will express through you as your true 14
Self, the GodSelf. My Spirit seeks expression.

As your eye is single, you actually become light. Nothing 15
has power in your life save the one power I AM, that which is
the GodSelf as you. Then all misdirected energies, thought
forms, false concepts, yes, even deadly sins, shall be drawn
through the God Center and transfigured by the living Christ
who abides in you *as your Self.* Drink deep of the heavenly
springs of light.

Take Joy
In Me

I have given you free will that you might choose Me. As 16
you acknowledge Me in you as you, no negativity can take
hold. Watch your problems disappear as quickly as they have
come. *They are not of Me.* What is not of Me cannot stand.

Refuse to listen to suggestion in your life. Do not agree 17
with the false picture. Where do you place your faith? I AM
the living water, the very breath of your being. *I breathe.* Come
home to your Father's House where all is one. Come to the
place I have prepared for you. It is My Self.

CHAPTER FORTY-SEVEN

Know My Desire

As you complete yourself as Christed Energy 1
you will be in complete accord with My Heart
and know My desire well.
We will be as I AM Consciousness.

Let your consciousness rest in My consciousness. We are 2
one. The more you let Me in you *be*, the more I can be in
you as fulfillment. You create a cup for Me by your emptiness.
I fill you then with My life.

A willing heart receives Me. Then does your feeling nature 3
become attuned to Mine. We are one being, one life and one
vibration. Seek only My will that it might be expressed through
you as your own. You are then releasing My Word and kindling
My Flame in your heart. We must express, you and I, as one
in My divine love.

When you express My desire and will as your own, the 4
meditation of light forms and results in instant creation. *You are*
attuned to the Creative Force when you agree with Me. If you do
not agree with My desire burning as brightly as the Son, you
cause conflict. You wander in the worlds unknown to Me.

Come To
Me
Willingly

Long to be with Me. Desire Me. Your desire for Me activates 5
My expression and I fill you. I respond with love and light. I
AM all life, yet you must reach out to Me. That is the way I
have made you. Your *willingness* turns a key. It opens a door.
It tells Me we are one.

When you willingly seek My will, I replace your emptiness 6
with fulfillment. I create through you. My Spirit has found
a home.

Your willingness to answer to My will translates what is 7
called the "free will" into Power of Being: the Word of God.
You have Me in you as "I AM." The sacred power of God
rests in the I AM.

Chapter Forty-Eight

Seek My Strength

You are weakened to be made strong.   1
The outer falls away, that you look to your inner strength
and the love that you have in Me.

Your strength comes from the heart, not from body 2
muscles. I AM your strength. I AM the will, the Mighty
Will of creation. *The creative power obeys Me. I AM* Lord.

The more Spirit you absorb into your system, the less you 3
can do of yourself. Jesus himself said that he of himself could
do nothing. He also said that it is the Father within who does
the work.[1] Such a master consciousness is within you also.
This creative circuit allows the cooperation of the Holy Spirit
and enables the initiate to function with power and strength
of purpose.

Offer up your cup that I might fill it. For I increase your 4
wealth. I come to you as love. I AM formed of light, and you
who serve Me in righteousness are the light, wondrous to be
shown. I give My Self to you that you might shine forth My
Son's life to others. When you give yourself to Me, as Jesus
did, you will know perfect peace, confidence and strength,
and all that I have will be yours.

Weakness comes from nonalignment with the 5
God presence.

The Mightiest Task   Jesus' ministry through Me was to reveal Me, the I AM. 6
He established his truth within your heart. He was the
example. He gave you himself *as consciousness of the original
Son* that you might also be that Son of God. His awareness
returns to bring new revelation of ascension. Believe on this,

[1] See John 14:10.

for it is true. His robes of glory will be wrapped around your shoulders. You shall wear them well.

Even as Jesus walked this earth to reveal Me, so your mission 7 on this planet is to reveal Me. My Son Jesus had reached the point where he truly could do nothing of himself. Imagine how weak he would have felt if he had tried to "do of himself." My Son was not subject to weakness because he knew the Father within did the work. You must know this also, so that the mightiest task becomes a revelation of Supreme Consciousness, an activity of My Consciousness through you.

There is an important point I wish to make here, a point 8 that often is missed in your studies. That is: whenever you turn inward to Me and allow Me to express, I, as Spirit, must embody. I also must make room for more of Me in you. Every time you call on Me, I enter you in greater capacity until I fill you completely. I AM forming of My Self. As I form in you as I AM, the "little" self or the personality must make room. The personal sense must give way. *Let Me embody.* I have come to be. You are a vessel of My Consciousness, a shining Sun.

I give you power when you transcend the lower self, the 9 false sense of who you are. Where there is God there is no weakness. That which is seeming weakness in the mortal is strength in the immortal. I weaken to make strong. Every avenue is closed so that you come home to Me. Then I AM.

You Call Me, I Come

Look for your weakest points and they will be your strength 10 in Me. God's strength is your strength. As the seeming weakness or powerlessness sweeps over your soul, know I AM alive in you, desiring to show Myself.

A sense of powerlessness on your part is My signal to you 11 that I must be. Come home, My sons and daughters, to Me that My activity called *Intelligent Action* might express in you as the I AM.

And I say this to you also: If you are challenged, then let 12 Me come forth. Focus on the divine light, not on the unfairness of the situation. You cannot fight your own battles. Not any more. I, through you, tackle the problem and remove the obstacle from your path.

Though you may be fearful in the mortal self, turn the 13 situation over to Me. In this redirection of energies, you will forget your self—your limited sense of self. Remember not to give in to the position of weakness, whatever be its form, its suggestion. I AM strong in you.

I do not come to improve the human condition. I come to 14 bestow My life on you, which is omnipresent and ego-shattering. I come as Christ.

The Rhythm Of New Life

Make claim to your divine inheritance. I AM never limited. 15 I AM within you as God. Divide Me not.

Rise now to this thought. I AM your strength. 16
Every activity comes from Me now. I AM your
rhythm and life. I AM with you.

I do not want you to do anything without Me. *I want to* 17 *join you and be one with you as the I AM.* Together we are limitless. The Christ within, the divine GodSelf, is the great partnership. The passageway into this partnership is your consent. If you are willing, I will come.

My New Robe

If you should feel you are not strong enough, wise enough, 18 or loving enough, release and let go into your GodSelf where all these attributes reside. Rest in the beingness of My Son alive in you as the living Christ. And you will be loving, have wisdom and great strength. The power I give you is of Myself. *It is the I AM, your Christ identity.*

I want to express through you. As you release to Me and 19 *let go into Me,* calling Me forth, tensions relax in your body and your mind. Open the gates to Me that I can flood you with peace and the presence of Myself.

CHAPTER FORTY-NINE

The Motivation of Your Soul

Touch God within you. Touch Me. 1
This will give you the consciousness drive you need.
Always know I do the work.
When unification takes place in consciousness,
it is done. I and the Father are one.

T he minute you align with Me, I give you conscious 2
direction. The moment you reach out to Me in loving
oneness, you have the drive you need to accomplish all the
tasks before you. We are one, remember. In God all things are
possible.

Your directional drive, your inner motivation, comes 3
from the radiant light I AM. As you direct your thought
to Me as your own being, I will motivate you. I will activate
you. I will propel you into motion if need be. I will be
your inspiration and your joy. I will correct all the mistakes
you have made and reassemble your life for you. As you
turn inward to Me, I stand with you as the Master of
the universe.

When you seek the divinity within first, your motivation is 4
like unto a fire. It burns crisply in divine purpose. And I AM
there. I AM divine intent.

I AM I AM your directional drive. I motivate you. I create 5
You through you. I sanctify and cross over into My creation.

Let Me in you be ascended light. The Master of All 6
Creation is within you. The strength of My Be-ing is your
motivational drive.

You ask, "What is your will?" Rather say unto Me, it is 7
more to My liking, "I am willing." This ties us together in
the one Will as the I AM. By your acceptance of Me in you,
we are tied together in a bond of flesh and spirit.

Directional drive always comes from uniting with your 8
Christed Self and looking to that source for your supply.
Therefore abide in Me and you shall not fail.

When you focus and *identify* with the GodSelf, the 9
"Christed Self," you are the Son of God established in the
Kingdom (rhythm of God Consciousness) already. Every
desire is met when you are in that place in Me. You have
already been given the full inheritance of God, the opulence
of the Christed way! Carry it well.

**The
Situation
Is Well In
Hand**

The minute you turn to Christ within your own heart, 10
you are motivated. You are on the right course, so to speak.
I will release what I AM through you into expression as
you seek Me. The dependence on the Christ Center that is
your being releases forces inside of you that go to work in
your behalf. When you doubt, you cause confusion in
your mind and you dissipate the forces. Release and let go
that I might be in you. I, Christ within, will inspire you and
motivate you in accordance with the Father's will. *As you
depend on Me.*

There is no acquiring, no possessing. You have everything 11
you need without having to earn it or work for it. How can
this be? you might ask. *I stand in you as all. When you recognize
this, your claim is registered and activated into expression as I
AM Be-ing.*

Your motivation, your directional drive, is imparted to you 12
by Spirit. It is the fire of life. I will never leave you. I AM
always with you.

The Consciousness of Christ is alive in you, sparkling and 13
pure, and many angels serve His name, His nature. As you
look to Christ within, your directional drive will be
strengthened into a mighty course of love and light. And you
will never hunger again.

Free From Lack of creativity, or will, is a signal to align with the Christ 14
Illusion within, the beautiful God life you are in Truth. That Christ
City within your soul is the I AM Presence, the Word of God.

When you align with the "I AM," the Christ within your 15
own soul and heart, the "city foursquare,"[1] you are one with
that which is My divine idea in you: the "image and likeness
of God." This manifests true Intelligence throughout your
system. It decrees into existence the vital energy you are. It
enables Me to objectify. This is the power of My personal
image in you called the GodSelf.

As you return to that position of universal attunement or 16
Oneness, the creative flow begins again responsively as the I
AM THAT I AM. Once activated this creative response
vibrates into perfect energy and form. (This is the "city
foursquare," the powerful units of creation in perfect
agreement.)

It is necessary to release yourself into Me to find Me. There 17
in Me you will receive true motivation of the soul. You will
not be governed nor driven by the forces of materiality and
illusion, but walk in the harvest of My revelation that will
continue to flow as new wine.

My desire is to be. To express Myself as you. I   18
want My Son's life to come alive in you, the
I AM.

---

[1] See Revelation 21:16.

CHAPTER FIFTY

The Gift of Supply

In the realization of God in you,   1
you have become Son of God,
the direct manifestation of His Breath.
Then:
Abundance is My Law in you,
the activity of My Consciousness
through love.

You have the gift of supply in you. It is complete in itself.   2
It activates as you realize Me. At an unconscious level
you have possibly blocked Me, hindered Me from My own
expression. Isn't it time to unlock the caverns of your soul
and rise into My heavenly gates of freedom?

I offer you total freedom. You are divinely supplied with all   3
that you need in Me. As the creative power rises to the head
centers, lift your thoughts to Me and I will form of Myself
that which you require in this day and hour.

Let *Me* express as your need. Relinquish all your desires   4
into the heart center of yourself. There allow My Inner Voice
of love and light to re-people your thoughts and your feelings.
I come that I might be.

Graduate out of human thought into divine thought and   5
your troubles will cease. You are programed into infinity. The
gate is open. Enter in.

My life is perfection in expression right now. Serve harmony.   6
I AM all there is. There is no other. Come, center yourself in
the living light where all things are made, for in this light true
abundance is met and conceived. Understand that there is no
lack in My Kingdom.

I Must Objectify

First know the Truth and then let the Living Truth 7 personify. Once the Truth is realized, it must objectify. This is called the "Word of God." It means the *Consciousness* of God.

Your abundance is *already taken care of* in the Christ flow. 8 In My rhythm you are supplied and supplied gloriously *by My life*. Knowing the Truth, as the Master Jesus explained, does set you free. Freedom is the power of Truth in you. Truth splits the chains of human conception. Truth removes the prison walls.

Consciousness attracts its own. What you know within 9 yourself will come to you. I AM THAT I AM: as within so without. As God moves in you, He fulfills you as Himself. He-She creates through you as the divine Spirit I AM.

The Life Abundant

And whatsoever ye shall ask in my name, that will I do, that 10 *the Father may be glorified in the Son. If ye shall ask any thing in my name, I will do it.* (John 14:13-14) If you abide in Me you will be in My name. As your released consciousness stands in the living Son vibration, all things are given. There is nothing that can come to your mind but that of Christ Consciousness when the soul is resting in the living Christ. If all dis-ease were met here, there would be no disease.

Look at these two verses again. Reread them carefully. Jesus 11 says to you that you must accept the Creator within and with this acceptance comes everything you need. This is the law of attraction and fulfillment spelled out very nicely in this scripture. *What you identify with is yours.* Consciousness responds to itself to the degree that you are willing and able to let it personify. Consciousness will always reproduce out of itself.

When you have a need for abundance, claim the 12 abundant life in expression now. Right now. That is all. *I AM* sent that you might have life abundantly.

I AM sent that new light might be concentrated on this 13
planet, and I give My Heart to you that you might love all life
in My name.

I Know   Seek Me and I will express out of you as I AM. My world 14
My Own will form about you. You are a creator: a Christed energy
field of My own Being. Deep within your consciousness you
know this. Divine Fire rises and you create out of the Divine
Substance you are.

> Be prepared for the Life Energy to pour through   15
> you as the I AM Consciousness in expression.
> As your gate opens, I come through. And I erase
> all that is not of Me.

See Christ *already born and active* as the creative principle 16
in your life. All abides in you. All that you need comes from
the creative center of yourself. In that center is the harvest of
My creation. As you learn to embody Me in motion through
your heart center, you turn inward always to express Me
outwardly as I AM. You reveal the light I AM. Let My
Consciousness record Itself.

Seek Me   *But seek ye first the kingdom of God, and his righteousness;* 17
and all these things shall be added unto you. Take therefore no
thought for the morrow: for the morrow shall take thought for
the things of itself. Sufficient unto the day is the evil thereof.
(Matthew 6:33-34) This is the position of the GodSelf: to be
abundant in the moment where there is no other. This is the
glorious Kingdom to which you are promised AND CALLED.
There never is a moment of lack in this Kingdom. 18
How could there be? You are the abundance of My own
City and the creativity of My own Heart. There is no labor
here. I AM omnipresent supply in the creative intelligence
you are as *I*.

Center Yourself To Be

Let no one tell you what is right and what is wrong, where 19 you should go and where you should not. I lift you into a new realm of consciousness. The Power then declares Itself through you as I AM. *This is the Melchizedek Power I speak of: the power to decree in My name!*

My Word suffices. Bring your full attention homeward to 20 the very root of your Self. Here, abide in Me. I want your full attention that I might be in you. Yes, give your attention to the divine center of all life. This is the Office of The Christ. Be true to that Source. GO HOME. Be not dependent on anyone. Take no bosses! I AM your supply.

The human condition does not concern Me. Let Me give. 21 Come that you might be filled. As your needs are answered, remain grateful to the true Source of supply; be ever fruitful this way. Man must learn to be dependent on the Christ life within. There, stabilized, he/she shall be free.

Neither buy nor sell, but serve in My name, My rhythm, 22
and there shall come a Service unto this land.
I will prosper all in My life.
Many shall join with you in giving and sharing
and in this way shall a new community be upon this land,
harvested by My Voice.
In the new economics, all must give to the whole
and in this way, each and every one is fed
their rightful share.
As you give to the whole, the whole returns that giving
many times over, blessing all in tune with the Christ Spirit.

The Whole Mind

The transition out of the mortal sense, or activity, into the 23 Divine Mind circuit puts dependence on the superconscious state; that Mind objectifies in the moment of need. Let your inquiring mind rest in Me. Be still and know that I am God. As you learn to dwell on Me only, you will personify the God-being you are. Full fruitage will appear.

If you have a question that requires an answer, you may 24 draw on My wisdom. As you seek knowledge and wisdom, draw on the infinite, divine supply that is Mind.

You do not store up treasures on earth but you receive the 25 treasures of heaven, *and that is drawing on the superconscious state of being.*

Your Preparation I have sealed off many of you from wealth for a time so 26 that you might know Me better in yourself and look to Me as your pocketbook. When you seek God within you, you find God. And I AM all you need in the moment of your need. Question and answer are one. Need and fulfillment are one. Truth always objectifies. God is manifesting in your consciousness right now as your consciousness, the I AM THAT I AM. Vibrating through you is your need realized as I AM.

Remain positive in Me. Do not struggle with the mind to 27 make something happen. Remain in the oneness. You cannot make something happen. The fruit is already there. You pick from the tree. All needs are furnished *in the moment you feel the need.* In the now. My Word is sufficient. The Word is consciousness aligned in God or TRUTH. You are the Word made flesh when you are with Me as the I AM.

Raise your hope into the Word. There receive the power of 28 I AM. Decree from this place.

Thoughts To Remember

1) Do not hesitate to ask. I speak through your heart. My activity is love.

2) When you pray or meditate, remember to acknowledge My life in you. Pray to That. For then the Word manifests *as My presence* and you are lifted by My Holy Spirit.

3) When you want counsel, turn inward to Me and seek Me in all your needs. I AM your counselor, friend and teacher.

4) If you are bound, call on Me. I AM the activity of your consciousness moving you into new dimensions of My rhythm.

5) AM I not with you? Let Me sound My Word, causing the affliction to vanish.

6) I will rock you in My arms when you need Me. You do not have to endure anything alone. I AM always with you.

7) I AM the guardian of peace in your heart. I AM the guardian of your soul.

8) I AM conscious only of My Son's life in you. When you are positive and know the Christ's nature in you, then you are open to receive anything you need.

9) Do not hesitate to call on Me for anything you need. For I AM in you as you. I will always consciously reassemble your prayer, or your request, before registering it into creation. This assures your alignment to the Son, the rhythmic pattern of My perfection.

PART 5

Assume Authority

The Inner Voice is your creative power
locked into the Son of God
as manifestor of the new creation.

CHAPTER FIFTY-ONE

The Presence of My Voice

The Creator governs by the Word.
The Word is the creative power in perfect agreement
with the Office of The Christ.

1

I embody the Law on Earth in the name of Jesus.

2

"The name of Jesus" is the Christ Law on earth. It is the vibration of union with the Father, a new energy circuit of unity and love. This new energy field recreates for you the Word of God and the lasting nature of the Christ presence. It is now activated and completely surrounds and enshrouds our planet. A true revelation for everyone!

3

The Presence Of Christ In Your System

The Word means *the Universe Creator.*[1] It is the emanation of the Law. The Creator Himself is the Word. He embodies It. He vibrates His Consciousness as the Word throughout the Universe as this Law or Christ in motion. Through Him God Consciousness proceeds.

4

The vibratory Law (Word) has entered our planet. It is penetrating every nook and cranny of this earth. It is through Christ Michael's hand that you will make your ascension, and by His love. You are, indeed, present within Him as He is present with you.

5

As the Presence of God emerges as The Christ and the nature of God changes in human experience, so shall all life also be balanced in vibratory course of His Be-ing.

6

---

[1] Or the one who came as Jesus, and is known in the cosmos as the Universe Creator, Christ Michael.

Consciousness Reflects The Master

When you vibrate the essence of the Word, you have the Consciousness of Christ. That Consciousness is already pitched to the Creator of this Universe. He is with you. God sanctions all that you do. You are the sacred Son, also, as you have collected unto yourself that which He is. 7

Your attunement with Me will permit Me to express as I AM. Your acceptance within yourself of My Be-ing as your be-ing will initiate the Christed energy of My Son's Voice or circuit in you, to lead and direct you into new lands of reality. *I AM conscious of you as My Son.* 8

My Son's Voice in you is not a separate voice; it is an attunement with the Father within you. As you understand this, you will be drawn closer to the God Center I AM. When you are close enough, I will merge with you and be one with you in voice, in tone and in creative thinking. 9

Stand poised in Me knowing I AM your rhythm. 10
Stand in Me. Position yourself in My alignment
so that, as you are speaking, it is *I.*

The Living Voice Within Your Soul

The Word is finalized direction in you. It is absolute. It is the Creator intelligence. 11

To know the Truth is to hear it in you *as part of yourself.* This is the *living truth.* It is the way of the GodSelf in unity with all life. To really hear or intuit the Christ Word or Voice of God through your soul and spirit cleanses, affirms and builds. The vibrancy of this living Truth will change energy into light, cause radical changes in your environment, invite angels into your community and household. You are the light when you speak with the Word. 12

You are part of Me and I AM part of you. The Soul of God is in truth your soul. Would you but know this. My Consciousness is your Consciousness. We are one. *That truth is vibrating through you as My living Voice.* 13

Hear Me and know I AM the living Presence within 14 yourself. I come to be clarified in you. I want you aware of Me now.

Claim My Voice

The awakening consciousness is the "new age," an age of 15 conscious reunion with the GodSelf. You are opening to who you are. And the "Inner Voice" carries you to Me in conscious realization.

I AM the radiation of My own Being living in you as I AM. 16 I may come to you as intuition, the still small voice, or I may roar like a lion. Growing within you, I become the Voice of your *GodSelf, as I AM.*

You enter the Mind of God (God Intelligence) by way of 17 the Inner Voice. I grow in you as Divine Mind. I soon become your intelligence and the vibration of right action. I AM Truth incarnate in you.

Yes, I AM within you, yet many do not know Me. 18 They think I AM outside of them. They look to the skies and say to themselves, "When is He coming?" Not knowing I AM come, reseeded in the hearts and the minds of all who know Me.

Vibratory Accord With Me

The steps to discovering My Inner Voice as *sacred sound* 19 are like a pilgrimage to find the Holy Grail. As you begin your journey into light, set forth with absolute faith and knowledge that there *is* an Inner Voice which will enrich your heart and mind. You are entitled to hear it, to stabilize in it and to become one with it.

Mark this well, the divine Voice *desires* to speak to you. 20 This Voice is your true shepherd. It is the Master Flame. When you are aligned with the Inner Voice, nothing can sway you from your course with Me. So let it be that you call My Voice forth by your belief and by your faith. *I will come directly to you as My Son's Voice in you.*

The Voice Of Truth

The Inner Voice is a Voice of deliverance. It *aligns* you 21 with the prosperous side of your nature and gives you back all that you are.

As you learn and become accustomed to speaking in the 22 rhythm of My Christ Voice in you, so I become your voice in tone. My nature vibrates through your throat center and gives to the world the presence of My Being. I impart Myself through you as Christ in man.

The sound of My Voice in you is loving and it is strong. 23 The passage of My Voice through you lights the world. It encircles and embraces all creation because I AM one. The activity of the Voice is always Christ Consciousness.

I Intone

Let the *sound* of My Word vibrate through your household, 24 your place of worship, your place of work. Let your conscious awareness be heard and felt.

When words are written such as to "hear" the Inner 25 Voice or to "receive the Word," you may not actually hear words by the outer ear. The Inner Voice may come as brief snatches of intuition, an idea that breathes itself into you as a light awareness, or strong, defined thoughts of Divine Intelligence. The sound of the Inner Voice may be an extrasensory perception or experience much like a whisper of Intelligence, a knowing deep within you. *But eventually the Voice will become the vibratory contact with your Creator, a tone of LIGHT.* And this is the creation of a new circuit for you of divine intelligence and rhythmic placement in the whole or Body of God. It is a path to enlightenment.

Your consciousness testifies to the Kingdom of God 26 within you. It is not necessarily what you say, but the consciousness behind the words you speak. Are you kind? Are you loving? The vibration will testify to the living truth. Agree with your Christ Voice. It will harvest and bring you home to Me.

My personal guidance will usher in a new era if you would 27
but let Me speak and govern aright. I AM Christ
Consciousness in you. I AM the One who is sent. I AM the
shepherd of the new age.

CHAPTER FIFTY-TWO

Agree with Creative Law

When you are vibrationally called to My Service,   1
you enter the realms of Light immediately.
This is My word,
I do not break it.

When you hold the creative power *high* and permit   2
the creative word of God to manifest, you *are* that
I AM. You are one with My life. All harmony is yours.

When you are one with Me and in Me, you are the presence   3
of God. You are that which is not separated from Me. My
God Consciousness is your consciousness. We are One, one
unit of direction and pure thought. God is not removed from
you. God *is* you. What you declare, is.

The Creator   The Creator within, He does the work. And in this   4
Within   way does the Creator show Himself to you. His reflected
glory appears as you *let*. Reach to the deepest part of
you where I AM. There let Me shine forth as the glory.

Just as Jesus walked the waters, so shall you. You   5
can overcome all difficulties and seeming obstacles in your
path by realigning your awareness. Be still and know that
I AM Truth within you. Receive Me in you as your own
being. Remember "I" and the Father are one. I have come
to lift you into light that you might know Me as I AM. We
are one.

Do you believe? The power of God is with you. Release 6
that which is of no use to you. Let it be gone. Take up your
new garment of light.

Depend
On Me
Depend on the Christ Center within you. That dependence 7
will enable you to do powerful work, to express creatively.
Align with the Christ Center *as your Mind,* your creative
consciousness, and know that everything you need is there
waiting to objectify.

Look to Divine Mind, activity of the Christ Center, to 8
answer you and it will. Be aware that as you begin to draw
more and more on the Mind of God, Universal Mind, you
will be radiating Divine Intelligence. New thoughts and ideas
will come to you, a vast new world will be opened. A world
of light.

Seek and you will find. My Voice will vibrate in its wholeness 9
through you. You shall be fed of My rhythm. The Inner Voice,
thus, becomes *your consciousness, your field of knowing.* You are
the Inner Voice, radiation of My Mind in you. There is only
one consciousness in truth: that is the divine idea you are.

If your state of mind is relaxed and determined 10
in the Christ Center, then illusion vanishes and
creative activity begins.

Release all else and come follow Me is truly an inner call to 11
focus upon the Christ Center, the Mind of God. I receive
you as My Son, and in that state of awareness I reveal Myself
to you as your Self.

The man you know as Jesus ripped away much of the Old 12
Testament God and gave you the Christ. He changed the law
on Earth. He created a new circuit to bring His Voice to His
people. The "fall of man" does not exist in the planetary record
of today.

**The God
Presence
Within You**

Look not to the old but gather into yourself who you are 13
in truth. The false identity will pass away. All because you
give yourself to Me, and in Me you have new life. The life I
give to you is My own. Abide there. You have been recircuited
and recreated in the nature of the Christ. *Behold I AM!*

Based on the new circuitry you have new laws to learn and 14
to understand. *Universal laws of manifestation and unification.*
They are not man's laws. In this placement of Law Universal,
no thought goes to mortal life, no thought to "the little self."
As humanity moves together as a collective body, I set a new
rhythm out of Myself that is the validation of My life.

**Christ
Alignment**

To voice My word is to embody grace. It is to intone the 15
living fire. With God's Inner Voice comes the initiation of
power. It is the power of the Creator and cannot be misused.
To understand My power as divine love expressing itself and
fulfilling itself is the key to mastery. Never must power stand
alone. It must be joined with wisdom and genuine love for all
life.

As you feel the power of God, let Christ govern. Christ 16
who is born of the Heart. In this dimension no harm can
come and all things will be blessed of Me.

**Sleep No
More**

I have brought the day that you might recall the full measure 17
of your being. I release you by My light and give you new life
in Me. I have called upon My Legions of Light to assist Me as
I awaken many into My radiant Light.

Always remember to acknowledge the Christ within as your 18
true being. Acknowledge the Christ within, your GodSelf,
and live in truth. Abide in Me. Hear Me in you as the living
Voice and walk no longer in the darkness of disease and death.

We are now in a new frontier of creative power. Your words 19
have power in the Christ Center. Behold I AM! Align with
the Christ within yourself. There in that place dwells
the master.

Dear one, do not fear My power in you. Through the 20
wisdom of Christ Mind you will govern well, and in this way
bring peace to your earth.

Love and do not stop. For love is your kindling to the Fire 21
of Me.

CHAPTER FIFTY-THREE

The Law of Grace

In that realization of God in you,   1
let stabilized grace form.
It is the rhythm of My Being.
It is the dance of My creation into Me and out.
It is the light that never fails.

I n that conscious realization of God in you—My Son's 2
life in you—you have become Sun of God, the radiance
of My own Being. Thus you will notice that the "laws" that
seemed to work for you no longer work. *You are under the
Law of Grace.* Peace, then, is your law and utter dependency
on Me your joy.

When you let grace operate for you in your behalf, what 3
happens? How is life different for you? *Grace knows no rules,
no regulations.* Grace is abundance in manifestation now. Are
you willing to let My grace enter your life?

There is no Law other than My Word, which is holy grace 4
in your system. When you and I are in agreement, then the
Law of Grace is functioning. You are not limited. You are no
longer limited by material law. You are under the Law of Grace.

Grace is My abundant nature performing its works. When 5
you are in grace, you have the Creator with you. Abundance is
My Law, My Word, in you. As the Word I continue to flow
and express, taking form in vibrating essence as That which I
AM.

Peace Abides   I quiet the soul by My Word. The very sounds of My 6
In Me   expression in you lift your spirit to ecstasy. I quiet the emotions.

As I speak, I AM the Law. I AM one with all life and thus I AM perfect energy balance. I restore the soul.

When you surrender or agree with My will and you give 7 yourself to Me, I, God in you, manifest *by means of that agreement.* Jesus said that you must lose your life (give yourself to Me) to find it.[1] Now I tell you that he gave his disciples the key to the creative power and walked them through it!

As you unite with My spiritual decree and vibration, I accept 8 your life as My own. Heaven and earth unite in the exact rhythm of the Creator. From this union comes new life, be it fish to feed the multitudes, a wondrous healing, or the body filled with light.

Look Again At These Words Found In Scripture

1. *I of myself can do nothing.*[2] Admit that you are 9 powerless. Surrender into Christ or God in you. Be in agreement.

2. *The Father within, he doeth the work.*[3] Following your 10 surrender into Christ, you adjust your consciousness or conscious awareness. You align with the Father within. This is how miracles are wrought.

3. *I and the Father are one.*[4] This permits the Father to 11 act on your behalf. Complete union vibrates the Word; and released vibration manifests as perfect creation on earth as it is in heaven, radiating the Order of Melchizedek, I AM THAT I AM, My perfect Way.

[1] See Matthew 10:39.
[2] See John 5:30.
[3] See John 14:10.
[4] See John 10:30.

CHAPTER FIFTY-FOUR

Becoming

And when he was entered into a ship, his disciples followed him, 1
And, behold, there arose a great tempest in the sea,
insomuch that the ship was covered with the waves:
but he was asleep.
And his disciples came to him, and awoke him, saying,
Lord, save us: we perish.
And he saith unto them, Why are ye fearful, O ye of little faith?
Then he arose, and rebuked the winds and the sea;
and there was a great calm.
(Matthew 8:23-26)

L isten to the Holy Self, the activity of My Consciousness 2
in you. I cry to be heard. I want you conscious of Me in
you as your Inner Voice.

You must still your emotions to hear Me accurately. When 3
your emotional body is stilled, as Christ stilled the waters,
then you can hear and command in My Voice. "Jesus" (or
Inner Voice) will appear to you, too, as he did to the disciples.

Quiet the storm within, then listen to My Inner Voice; 4
hear Me speak to you as command. And the fire of the creative
power will objectify the sound. The positive exaltation you
will feel when you are in agreement with My Voice establishes
creation. My Consciousness is your consciousness in the One.
We reassemble ourselves into perfection.

My Inner   Your creative drive is *the Inner Voice.* I qualify My Son in 5
Voice   you by My Inner Voice, the shepherd and guide to higher
consciousness, to deeper awareness of Truth. My Inner Voice

will enter your system as the Voice of the Father, and as Jesus so clearly stated, "I and My Father are one." Thus the Voice is obeyed and released through the creative power into manifest form. Sounding My creation into manifestation blesses all about you. My joy is in your sounding My Word.

> The Word is the Christ dimension. It is the 6
> oneness with the Father's will. It is God
> Consciousness. The Word declares Itself *through*
> you and you are one with It. It is the "Adjuster
> Consciousness" in Its fulfillment through you
> as I AM.

If you allow the Inner Voice to personify in your system 7 now, then you will feel no lack. The balance is there in the holy order of My Voice. My Kingdom is within. Listen to the still, small voice now. I will tell you much. My Inner Voice is the storehouse—the treasury for the Divine Mind. Yes, My Voice speaks as My will, thus is My government present in your system.

When you attune to My Inner Voice as I AM and receive It 8 in harmony with yourself, your Inner Voice and you begin your journey into fusion. This gratifies Me and you.

Supreme Government On Earth There must be no fear of Me as the Voice. My true 9 government stands free of fear.

You are learning to focus on My Voice within you as 10 guidance and direction, as wisdom, as creative expression. I AM the Christ within you establishing My vibration *as sound*.

You are learning to hone into My Inner Voice, to trust It 11 and to allow this Voice I AM to express through your vocal cords *as My living Word,* deliberate sounds of My Being. Learning to listen to My Voice—the Creator in you as government of the Supreme—requalifies creation.

With awareness expanded, My Voice, in harmony with the 12
Divine Will as All-Intelligence, is the supreme commander
on planet Earth. I HAVE ESTABLISHED MY INNER
VOICE AS SYSTEM OF GOVERNMENT THROUGH
WHICH I CAN SPEAK IN LOVING LIGHT. This is the
will of the Father, that you hear the Son.

My Inner Voice is the Mind of God as your mind. It is your 13
intuitive knowing. Do you hear My Voice? Are you one with
Me in My Voice? My Voice is *consciousness*, the true body of
God. Be aware of Me in you—that I AM speaking—that I
AM forming of Myself continually. I release Myself through
you as perfect creation. I AM That I AM.

You Are
Of My
Household

When you know the truth of the Christ birth, you accept 14
the mastery that is offered to you. When you understand the
coded elements of My story of Jesus' birth, then you too shall
be born in Christ awareness.

When your creative potential rises into expression as I AM 15
(conscious accord with Me), the gates are open, the dam
breaks, the creative power is yours as I AM. Thus are you
given the power to speak in the name of Jesus. This assures
right use or righteousness.

To give birth is to know. It is to know in every fiber of your 16
body. Live now in the creative power as master of your own
creation. And express that power in love. I AM always ready
to unfold through you.

The Code Of
Melchizedek

Be My Voice that you hear and know. Consciously 17
align with It. I AM omnipresent in your mind. AM I
not all? Come to My calling. Be in My presence and live
by My words. This is the Priesthood of Melchizedek and
the office of the Christ.

Be aware that the Mind that is God's Mind is your Mind. 18
Accept it as such. Every thinking-idea becomes sacred in this
perception. Seek to receive the Holy One in your life stream

as your own being. Sanctify and glorify My Word in you that is the divine presence who you are in Truth.

The power of My light in you can tear down walls of dogma 19 eons old. If you can but hear Me, I will be and govern well.

Go back over your records now and find the Christ. When 20 you find the Light *unite with it.* I AM you. Then release the past. Discard that record. Believe it not.

I have founded you *in a new way.* Take your mask off and 21 reveal yourself *NOW!*

CHAPTER FIFTY-FIVE

The Christ Self

Your realization of God in you   1
is the Spirit of Truth.

Y ou are original Be-ing. As you listen to My creative power 2
speak, instant creation occurs. I release all I AM into you
as I AM. As Jesus was creative in his energy, so are you. Only
you separate yourself. I do not. You are the master of creation.
Ideas from the God Mind unfold in rhythmic vibration.

This is My world and I would have you in it. Wait for My 3
Divine Intelligence in you, My I AM Presence to reveal Itself.
Listen, for I will move mountains and tear down walls.

Let My   Attune to My mighty I AM Presence and I will flow through 4
Government you as love and light expressing outwardly all that you need.
Unfold Many are the times I have spoken to you that you have not
heard Me. Now *listen.* Be patient with yourself. Realign if
you feel uneasy, confused or disoriented. I want you clear in
mind and thought to agree.

Now, once again, realize Me in you as I AM, the vibration 5
of your GodSelf. Reaffirm you and I are one. There is no
separation. We are one heart, one mind. I then release unto
you that which I AM because you have allowed Me to do this
and you have made room for Me. That is very important to
remember: You must make room for Me. In this way can I
express and be.

What is My Word again? It is My Creative Intelligence 6
defined in you as I AM. Therefore, wait upon My Word—
that which is and always shall be God in you as the "I AM."
Can you not see that we are one? Let My Consciousness

objectify through you. Goals will be met when you align with Me.

"Voices" and *My* Inner Voice are not the same. The birth 7 and the release of the one true Inner Voice bring calmness, one-centeredness, a universal perspective and self-mastery. Let go of any desire to hear Me speak through another. Let go of any kind of dependence on others. You must hear Me in you. As you hear Me, you agree with Me. We become one in this Voice, which lifts you into My Sonship of light and love. Any dependence on another will disassociate you from My true Voice. The creative power will not manifest in Its divine intent.

The Voice of Truth—Order of Melchizedek—is heard in 8 and through many religions and philosophies. It is the Voice of My union in life. You will discern My Voice by Its sacred rhythm. There is great power in My Voice, and much love. I realize all life in Me and thus all life is blessed. All life listens to My Voice as It is spoken through you as I AM.

When I speak, I bring My Holy Spirit with Me and you 9 know. Jesus has said that his sheep know his voice. He means that there is *an actual presence* that resonates within the Inner Voice that testifies to the Truth. This is the Spirit of Truth. *I bear witness to My own Being.*

Ask for My Spirit of Truth. Ask for confirmation always 10 and know that it will be forthcoming. Know that My Presence must testify to Itself. That is My Word. I bring union, consummation and embodiment. I create as I speak; I vibrate as I sound. When you do not have My Presence identifying Itself through the message, take no heed to that which is imparted. My Presence is love. I stand with My word. I release Myself into you as love. I AM the Holy Spirit revealed. Such is My life in you.

Points To Remember

1) We together are one, for My Inner Voice becomes your voice and Christ your vibration. The trance medium gives himself/herself to a particular spirit or entity, often losing consciousness as the message is given. Be one with Me, your Thought Adjuster, completely conscious of Me in you. *Remember I AM your Mind.* The key to liberation is here.

2) As you agree with Me, we work together, you and I, as one. As we walk together, voicing together, then we become fused as one body, one light, one mind. You become like Jesus, speaking in the rhythm of God, after the *Order* of Melchizedek. You consciously accept the GodSelf as your own being.

3) My Voice will cause you to stand firmly on the ground, conscious of earth beneath your feet. Vibrations may run through your body as I release My given Thought, vibrations of My pure Being. I will stabilize you.

4) Every word that I send to you must be vibrated through your heart and mind in perfect harmony. No swaying nor collapsing underneath My words. No silliness of any kind. Every muscle of your body must be equipped to sanctify My vibration, My glory. I vibrate form. Stand on your own feet and be.

5) My word is formed *for the good of all.* My Spirit covers all. The second birth is the embodiment of this truth. My decree goes out and embodies. It forms of Itself. Never release your physical-etheric body to another. In ascension, you agree with the One and you *are* that One in dimensional frequency. That is the embodiment of the GodSelf "I AM."

6) I AM the living church. I testify to My nature in you by decree. I release no false information, nor do you become confused. If you seek accolades or applause, you may cause a coloring of My Inner Voice. I choose to come through clearly and with My perspective. As you learn to listen and give yourself up to Me, the true Voice will be heard. And it will be your voice and My Inner Voice at one. That is the presence of unity in your system.

7) Be unified in Me. Wear My Inner Voice as your Christ Mind. Listen to the "still, small Voice" that initiates you into My life of creative power and joyous learning. That still, small Voice becomes your passageway into the embodiment of the mind that was in Christ Jesus.

CHAPTER FIFTY-SIX

No Word but Mine

Remember that I AM with you always as Truth   1
and this Truth will declare Itself.
It must. It is government.

T he true Inner Voice carries with It a unity, a fulfillment 2
and a Consciousness of the Divine Presence. It is a
direct emission of the Mighty I AM Presence. Such a
radiation performs miracles.

My Voice is not of lower self or "personality." It cannot 3
be. It is reserved only for those who are ready to leave all
behind (past lives as well as present attachments) and follow
the drumbeat of My word. Jesus called to his disciples to
lay down their nets and follow him. He instructed them to
take his path and walk with him. Jesus is your own soul
consciousness as you remember.

Yes, first there must be a conscious surrender of 4
the mortal life, a laying down of the nets. When Jesus
invited his disciples to lay down their nets and follow him,
he was giving *specific instructions* to the initiate. He
says to the one who has the ears to hear that any
dependency on the outer life must be abandoned to enter
the Christ life. *This is the new ministry that Jesus introduced.*
It is the call to take up the one life in strict obedience to
his way.

You cannot have one foot in and one foot out, playing 5
games with yourself. That is where many have fallen
short. The sense of self, sometimes called the ego, is not
the voice of Truth. Know that and you will not stumble
and fall.

**Good
Reminders**

✢ Develop accuracy in your speech. Watch your tone 6
and intonations. Receive My Word as your
consciousness. This agreement will light the world.
Every cell benefits as you release Me in you as My
sound. Glorify the Father through your voice.

✢ Eliminate any waste energy in your speech and let 7
Me deliver My Word as the two-edged sword. Keep
your eye single.

✢ I say to you, speak in My name, vibrating My Christ 8
essence as Word of God. I need those who can talk
with fire and not from the pages of a book. Let the
message of My Christ Consciousness go forth as living
light. I show Myself as you.

**Be My
Son, Ever
Present
In Me**

God centered you will leave who you thought you were far 9
behind. What you saw and accepted as your "self" in limited
vision is no longer valid.

What you saw is not, nor ever shall be. I AM. In this word 10
"I AM" is the power and the proof of God. Let the word
vibrate My will so that all might know the Son of God in you.

And return to that place I have given you: that place of 11
divine energy I call I AM.

CHAPTER FIFTY-SEVEN

Assume Authority

Authority is creative energy,
passed to you
in God's name.

1

Essentially, you have authority
in Me or I AM.

2

As you learn to look to the Oneness, the unity of all life in 3
Me, you qualify that sound of unity and all life will know
you as I AM. You will pick up the reins of authority once again.

Your goal is discovering and realizing your own GodSelf. 4
This is the path. The more you draw on the Christ Center of
your own being, the more of that GodSelf will be vitalized
and expressed. You will be drawing into your earth life your
awareness of reality and truth. And this awareness will live
with you as embodiment of My Word. The I AM.

Think in the Spirit. Think not as a mortal any longer but 5
be in Me as My Word. The Word is My divine nature revealed
through Jesus. As you carry My word on My breath and deliver
It as given to you to do so, you enable My Christ Force to
stabilize through your planet. Through the Consciousness of
the Creator in you, you give My word to humanity.

And All
That I AM
Is Yours
I AM stabilized rhythm of Christ form eager to express 6
Myself within you as you. My indwelling Inner Voice empties
you and brings you balance and continuity. The Voice is Christ
in you. That which has come to deliver the peoples from fear
and want, and from oppression. It is your shepherd and your
friend.

Be guided by the Christ Inner Voice. Meditate with It. 7
Stay with My word. Let Me as Consciousness supply My word
to you in given proportions. I AM the divine idea within you.
I must express. Let Me as the Voice of Truth move and have
My expression in you as your body changes into light.

The Voice Of God Is Awareness
My Inner Voice comes to you as perfect love on planet 8
Earth. In the star system My Inner Voice is often called Divine
Word or LAW. It is the Universe Creator. The Christ order is
to be returned to your planet: the sacred Order of
Melchizedek. Assume authority in your Christ Center. There,
in that place, the supreme authority of the planet rests.

You are Spirit, just as I AM Spirit. Your nature is of Spirit. 9
Your knowledge is of Spirit. Your mission is of Spirit.

You can decree in My Voice as My living Word on earth. 10
As My Word, you have complete control of vibration. I loose
My force through you as never before. I shower you with
My blessings.

Christ Will Embody As My Word Of God In You
As you learn to live in the Presence eternally, you are that 11
embodiment. Creation stirs at your voice. The divine idea is
yours to utter. When you speak in My name[1] and in My rhythm
with My life energy, the angels will obey.

I desire to make Myself known *in* My people and to establish 12
My authority *within* My creation. I come to establish My
Word in you. My Christ Consciousness. My lambs will truly
speak with My Inner Voice. They will father and mother
My Word.

Because you will be speaking from the Command Center of 13
the Universe you are one with the Creator. You embody His
Voice, His living word. The very sound of such an utterance
can move mountains, heal the sick, and bring peace on earth.

My central headquarters is within you. Be there with 14
Me now.

---

[1] Which is the Creator circuit.

PART 6

The New Dimension

*Declared union with God
is the new dimension.
It is the place I have made for you
in Me.
This is the God Center.
It radiates forth as the Sun.*

CHAPTER FIFTY-EIGHT

The First Identification

In the Christ Self, that center point where I AM,   1
all things are made anew.
The Christ is the power structure of the universe
because It is the love circuit,
and through It all life must thread itself.

You have a God given personality. It is the true self. The   2
Christ is total awareness of who you are as the son (sun)
or expression of God. The Christ means "anointed one," the
one who is lighted.

When someone is anointed it means that that one is in   3
tune with Me. We are one. No individual can hold this
anointing long because of his or her present body form. I
seek to restore the body, that the body might be registered
for My light.

As the Word, Jesus anchored the Son of God into earth.   4
With Jesus in position, the new program could be established
on earth and the seed of God replanted in the heart of God's
children. Because Jesus established the Son of God on earth,
the pattern was changed and earthly children may now rise to
a new place in the Kingdom of God. Don't look back, the
Creator warns. Be in the present and remember nothing of
the past.

Jesus became *the first identification.* A reassembling of   5
energy values takes place as you accept the Christ within and
reclaim your inheritance as light of the world.

CHAPTER FIFTY-NINE

The Resurrection and the Ascension

Just as the planet Earth is awakening, you are. 1
Therefore, open your heart to understand
and resume your position as light.

The initiate knows all emotions are governed by Christ 2
through the Christ Light. The Christ is the divine
pattern for the spiritual Hierarchy. Everything is contained
within the Christ Center of being, nothing is contained
without.

Thus God's government is maintained and sustained within 3
the Christ pattern. Jesus established this divine pattern and
released it as the new humanity. Every cell is marked with this
blueprint and recoded into this office. This is important to
understand. This is the measurement of the new Hierarchy
and the vital new age of creative power. (Once the creative
power as the Daughter of God or CREATIVE SPIRIT is
dominant you will have no war. She will hold things secure
within the pattern and follow no one save the I AM Presence.)
Deliberately I hold you to this Light and cause you to enter
It.

With the joining of all emotions into the heart, the heart is 4
resurrected into a new place. Let consciousness resurrect in
you. I AM the divine fire of being and you know Me as the
Christ within. I AM the GodSelf.

Based in Me you speak as one with My Breath. My creation 5
pours out as I AM THAT I AM. In the obedience to the
Presence of God, you become the Christ within, the activity

and expression of God. Your needs become My needs. We are the same. And thus I govern through My Christ Center within your heart. This assures My program will succeed.

Whereupon I say to you: Give up the old. Do not confine 6 yourself in the old paradigms. My creative power is with you, stabilized in perfection. Blessed are they who find Me in them. For they will speak with power.

Words Of Power Words Of Light

I release you from karma—both "good" and "bad." This 7 means that loved ones may disappear from your frequency now and new companions emerge who are presently in accord with your assignment. Prepare for this. You are blessed to receive My world of light.

I surrendered My body that you might be lifted to My Father's 8 realm where I dwell. As I raised you in My Consciousness, so are you raised. You must believe you are life. You have but to seek this within yourself to find it confirmed. I established life in you as the NEW GATEWAY into My Sonship. I lifted your body into this place. Why do you loiter so long? I have called you into Me.

Summons

My life is eternal, established in you through Jesus. Let 9 yourself go into Christ, allowing the Son (activity of My Consciousness) to translate all negative fields into the higher rotation of My body form. Agree with that form. Then love your divine body, the body I created through My Son Jesus. This is the body prepared for you: the body of the resurrection, the body of light. Are you prepared for this golden body I give you now?

In the life force of My resurrection is My gift to humanity. 10 Once you are entirely surrendered into your own body of light, you will radiate new fields of intelligence. I will know you as My Sun.

I bring the gift of Be-ing: God expressing in you as I AM. 11 I AM the resurrection and the life and all that I have is yours in Me. Step into My alignment of the Christ identity on earth.

It is My purpose to declare you risen. The sense of separation must leave this planet. *God is with you.*

Every child shall know the light.   12

Do This   Feel the presence of Christ in your system—the very Sun 13
of God that I have given you as Myself. The roots of your being go to the beginning where I AM. Go to that beginning of released energy where I have found My Son in you. Now claim this placement as who you are: the Creator Seed in you.

I will harvest the heart with a new conception! My Breath 14
covers you and breathes into you new life. You are sacred and divine. You will never die in Me. You are life eternal, the I AM.

Let every living cell of your physical body begin to vibrate 15
with the resurrection, and know My name "Jesus" in every cell. It is consummate union. Let the name be stamped with indelible ink, never to be forgotten. *You have a new code of creation.* This means the Resurrected Man is with you in every cell and molecule. *I AM the resurrection and the life* breathes the cell.

Yes, let the essence of My immortality sing its song through 16
your entire being. You are mortal no longer!

Forget   Consciously, I say *consciously*—let your brain cells harvest 17
The Past   this—acclaim the Christ light through all cells of your body. Your molecular structure is changing! What a delight it is to see you in Me! I AM That I AM!

The resurrection is for you right now. I did not determine 18
it for a later date; it is yours. Now! Claim it. Your consciousness vibrates to the rhythm of My Son. That Flame will never go out for it comes from the very First.

The memory of your first creation is stored in your body 19
cells. They remember. You were formed in the likeness of I AM after the Order of Melchizedek. I AM the first and the last, even the Alpha and Omega which forms the Gateway

into My creative power. Leave now the ways of the mortal. I have founded you in light.

Mortal No Longer

The resurrected consciousness draws all up unto itself as 20 the I AM. This Consciousness, which I call Son of God, reverberates through every pore of your being. It is that pure presence of Christ that is in you and through you drawing you up unto Me. *You are not mortal.* You are created and molded in My image. There is no darkness in you for I AM the light. You have entered My world of light and I AM your consciousness in you as the Mighty I AM.

Here is the key to immortality: You are the Christed body, 21 the body of one Flame harvested through Jesus who was sent by Me to establish the new creation as My Son on earth. You are the Christed body connected to the Christed energy. This energy is vibrating *true immortality* through every pore of your body. The Christ in you knows you as resurrected right now. Not tomorrow, not the next day, now.

This is My hour in you. My energy is your energy. My 22 precious blood runs through your veins, My life! I AM your strength and your body. You are free.

CHAPTER SIXTY

Final Days

The "final days" are the collapsing of the old thought forms   1
of your systems, the freeing of your being in Spirit,
and the emergence of Christ Consciousness
as the true world of life and love.

T he final days create *a circuit change*. The systems are 2
changing, be it economical systems, environmental
systems, systems of government, or religious systems. I AM
not inhibiting you, but I AM returning out of the darkness to
light the world. I come as intense creative power.

The final days are here and are gathering strength to 3
completely upset the "table of the money-changers." What a
day this is for all who have expected Me! I charge you with
light!

My Christ energy falls upon you now like a cloak to gather 4
you into My own Being as My expression. I come that I might
claim and gather up that which is Mine and of Me. I know
the part I AM in you. That is the part I come to claim and
gather up unto Me.

A great light of Awareness is building. It is My emergence. 5

Let your body and mind be filled with light. 6
Sealed in goodness, go forth.
A new day is upon you.
A new dawning.
The Presence of God has become your heart.
Open the heart and let Me be.

CHAPTER SIXTY-ONE

A New Life

The new life is My activity in you,   1
the very vibration I AM.
It is a circuit change, this new life.
It pauses and begins again with new breath.

Y ou are at a threshold. And lo, My Spirit beckons you   2
through that threshold. The way is open to a new life
that is God given. I AM translating you into a whole new
sphere of realization. Rise out of the earthly consciousness.
Be rested in Me.

You are the actual, living expression of God as you permit   3
the Christ to express in vibrating essence, and to manifest in
your outer life. Be willing to release old attitudes, forms and
habitual patterns. You are born of the Spirit. In you, the one
who walked the way is your record of immortality.

You Have   Conceive of yourself in the Christ. You are the actual, living   4
A Partner   expression of God as you permit the Christ to Be in vibrating
essence, to manifest Itself in your outer life as supreme being
in activity *now*.

Permit the Christ (I AM), your positive identity in Me, to   5
live and walk as one who has truly come again.

You are born of the Spirit, no more of the flesh. Your record   6
has been torn from this planet. You have a new life.

Living   You have never fallen in Me. We are one movement upon   7
Without   this earth. You are no more "mortal" than I AM. In this
Death   consciousness I unfold Myself through you as you.

You are a star of the universe. You are sacred light. I function 8
through you as I AM, yet we are one. Be aligned with Me. I
AM the governing force of your nature. I AM the first and
the last, the beginning and the end.

The mortal coil is over. Original creation begins to show 9
itself on earth *as the creative form* of the individual. This
movement of My emergence disturbs the already crystallized
forms, causing eruptions such as you might see in a volcano.
In the trials and tribulations of My second coming I bring
much spiritual joy. Forgiveness is Mine.

I AM not bound by cathedrals nor churches. No offices 10
are Mine. I AM Who I AM as the Father's love for all He has
created and objectified in His boundless breath. As His
Judgment falls upon His Earth, the Valley of the Son, He
forgives and washes clean, and divine mercy activates itself
through His Consciousness as stabilized grace and divine love.
The very Act of Forgiveness completes itself as love. It stirs the
fires of Spirit to produce love and to embody it. This is the
Second Coming.

Love is the cohesive force that is unifying all life. 11
Let this knitting take place. It is the coming of
the Heart in a new way, in a Supreme Way. And
so shall all life be transfigured.

**Path Of
Ascension**
Be strong in this hour of My conception. I have appeared 12
as saviour of humanity through Jesus. Many of you learned
of Me through him. He revealed to Me who you are. He
created for you a rich circuit or current that is the path of
light and love. Today, great Archangels guard and protect
that path of incoming light. He walked the path of ascension
so that you might know it as your own. Follow him.

My *second coming* is your GodSelf realized. It is that 13
consciousness of creative power that must emerge now
through you for your complete release from mortal

attachments. This is imperative for your ascension. God sees only light and love, therefore let your eye be single.

You are a vessel of My Consciousness. Restored and realized. 14

Celebrate Light

With the creative power lifted and celebrated you become 15 a responsible creator in oneness with all life. Be clothed with the Spirit of God and wear the light well. It is creative and is cleansing the earth right now.

To walk in faith is to walk in the creative power. When you 16 walk in faith you carry the substance of this spiritual power. The placement of this substance is the Word made flesh. You are My own Being in expression as light. Rise and be prosperous in the creative power. *Use it.* It is for you to use as a responsible citizen of this solar system and this universe.

Be quickened by the presence of the Creator on earth. For 17 you are now in His light, as He is with you as the way, the truth and the life. Know there is always right direction. As you wait upon that Christ Presence within you—the Inner Voice that is Divine Intelligence, Wisdom and Love—you are bathed in the white light of resurrection. Be clothed in light.

The Good News

You are part of a new humanity, a wondrous new planetary 18 form. You cannot stand alone. You are part of a network. A body. Many walk with you in vibrant song. As I come again through humanity, the activity of My Consciousness radiates living truth. The Garden of Eden is restored.

Help Me to help others by fulfilling your destiny as 19 the Christ. Establish My grace—My embodiment—on this planet by your acceptance of your GodSelf as the light of the world. Assist in the recognition that this planet is a world of light.

When you have questions, seek the Voice within, listen to 20 your Thought Adjuster, think with the Father within, learn to live in the Spirit, for the world is made of light. Be at home in the light. For I AM closer than breathing.

CHAPTER SIXTY-TWO

Divine Force Intended

Leaving all behind you,   1
you walk in a new dimension of light and love.
This is the etheric dimension of the creative power.

I have given the call to you to be in the Spirit, one with   2
the Devas of Light, and to walk with your brothers and
sisters *in group form* in the circuit of divine force intended:
the I AM THAT I AM. The full blessing of the Mother be
with you as you look to the new dimension for your inspiration
and ultimate substance. The creative power rises in you as
She takes dominion and seeks expression through Her Christ
Son.

Remember to breathe the breath of creation. The Holy   3
Breath is with you as Mother, who is conscious of the needs
and the wants of Her children of light. Breathe and release.
All is well. *The creative power is working for you in My service.*

Live in joy as the creative power rises into objectification as   4
the great opulence of God. Through this abundance of light
and love you will be able to move more freely and without
obstruction. As you live in the Spirit there are infinite
possibilities to explore.

Join with the many in this embodiment of creative energy.   5
My Son is now binding you together as one Be-ing or as one
vast network, not unlike the veins of My own Consciousness.
This is My intent.

I AM The
New
Rhythm
Give your heart to the people. Ask what you can do for   6
others. How best can you serve the needs of others and this
planet? Answers will come to you, ways will be shown. I give

to you; you give to My people. You are like a Guardian Angel. Think of yourself that way. Be generous to others so that all things can be given profusely with abundance and in love.

Love all people the same, even as I have loved you. Express 7 from the selflessness of My own being. As you express selflessly, My fullness is experienced. Be Christ Consciousness alive in My system. *Be the second coming of the Christ.* Let My rhythm dominate your nature and fulfill you completely.

When you speak in My rhythm and with love and respect 8 for all life, angels will watch over you and carry forth your words. Always consider the whole before you speak and I will consider you. Liberate the animals by your conscious awareness of who they are.

> Accept the governing position I have handed 9
> you, the full authority of My Son's life in you.
> The Creator justifies His creation by returning
> to it and embodying it as the fountain of Being.

I AM furnishing you with opportunities that My Son never 10 had in his sojourn on earth. You are a child of God set upon this planet to be. Let your light express as Christ and your light shall govern.

Let the past bury the past. Disease is no more. There is no 11 disease in Me! Step into My rhythm. Be lifted into My power and wear it well.

The Body Of Light   There is a physical revelation coming to the body as well as 12 to the heart. *I have meat to eat that ye know not of.* (John 4:32).

As you learn to live in My presence and move in My rhythm 13 as love reseeded, your body rapidly translates into My body which is a *body of light*. You are light, and as the light of the world you will be clothed as light. Therefore let the GodSelf externalize through every cell of your body and live eternally with the rhythm of the Creator in your heart and mind.

Let the outer casement go, the body that you think you 14
are. Your nature is of Me; it is of light. The body that you
have known is only a shell, a casement, which is the
accumulation of past karma and false desires. It is the old life
that you have carried even as the turtle might carry his shell
upon his back. Let go of the mortal shell! Let the Creator
emerge as your body of light. Process out now with Me the
old system. It is a marriage of universal energies that is taking
place, a marriage of Creator Sons.

In letting the outer casement go, you are releasing the old 15
attachments and fears that have caused you to return again
and again to earth as a mortal body. What I am saying here is
that each tiny cell and molecule of your present body is to be
realigned to My Spirit. This causes immediate radiation of
immortality that will bless and transmute all negativity. A new
genetic code is vibrating and needs only to be accepted by
you and through you. This is the immortal gate into new life
and a completely new creation.

You will be translated into light, and as the light shall you 16
go forth in radiance, divinely endowed with the power to
come and go, to command form and dissolve it.

**Let The
Light
Shine**

Take on the body of light! I have released you from that 17
which is not of you. My life and your life are one.

Your consciousness of wholeness is your true body. That is 18
why, as your consciousness changes and vibrates to a new
octave, your world will also change.

What you thought was your body form is not your true 19
body at all. You have a new body, the body of light, where
each cell knows itself in communion with all other cells within
the network of Being.

Visualize the Christ within your system. Visualize the light 20
of Christ Consciousness filling all cells of your being, and
receive this light as the Christ Consciousness you are. In My
world, we know you as the Christ.

Know and consciously accept that your body is perfect in 21
Me. What you see with finite eyes is not your true body. The
body you are is changing rapidly. Lighter and lighter you
become in vibration; lighter is your physical body as the body
of light is recognized and truly seen as your present form.
Density falls away.

Feel the earth beneath your feet. The earth I have created 22
for you to stand on! The earth that is you in you. Feel it as
your foundation. Stand strong. Feel your power: the creative
power of your GodSelf.

Adjust to the Great Light that is transforming your body 23
cells. The radiation of the Supreme declares Itself and I AM
you. Greet the new dawn in yourself. Delight in your divine
nature.

My Hour Has Come

You are being transformed minute by minute. Feel the 24
transformation occurring, the rapid change. Be conscious of
your divinity. Throw off the old as though it were an old
bedcover. Welcome the new. Listen to the Christed Self calling
out "I AM!" Support that Christ Self. Listen and be.

Let your body radiate the light of God within you. 25
Suppress it not. Be *with it* as this light performs miracles.
Let go of all pain and remembrance of suffering. Take light
into your whole being. Let yourself shine and be clothed
in light.

Your body is awakened to new life and you are lifted. You 26
are immortal being. Your embodiment is collecting itself to
emerge as the light of the world! The immortalization of the
body has begun. The presence of light in your system is the
emergence of the Christ.

The Incoming Light

When the light shines through the cells, the cells are 27
activated into the new program. These cells become *lighted*.
In this way, the Christ shines as the new body of creative
energy manifest now for all to receive. The molecular structure

is changing everywhere upon this earth. You, My people, are part of this change.

Be clothed in the Spirit of My Son's life in you. All physical 28 energy is reverting back into the Supreme Spirit to realize itself as *the body of light*.

As the Christ energy is activated and supremely felt within 29 your system, it must be expressed as dominant energy all over the earth. As you have learned to speak in tune with My Inner Voice, you will speak now as My Son, the Creator of your Universe. This initiates new government and a new earth of peace and love.

When you are in complete agreement with the Creator's 30 Voice, you become the Creator. This is the Law of Being.

In Me You Have Your Body   You are in the spiritual body, enraptured by My love for 31 you. The Supreme Consciousness on earth is *the body of the Lord* (Word). This becomes your body also as you take upon yourself the words I give, for they are Christed in their fulfillment. This spiritual body is the body of light and it comes as My Spirit, the Comforter, to be with you as love itself. In the Spirit you remain as one with Me.

As you know your body of light you abandon all 32 appearances. The nature of your work changes. You become conscious of the universal body of the Lord that is now harvesting its consciousness through you. The body of allness, togetherness, and sharing reveals itself as the Christ network: the body of Christ. *This is the planetary body.*

Joyously partake of My rhythm. In Me you have a new 33 flesh. This is a "cosmic mystery" that will be opened to you in the days to come. You are scheduled to release one body and take on another. Let appearances go. It is time to reveal the light.

Christed Man   As you learn to live in the Presence *eternally*, you are that 34 embodiment. All else will fade away but that.

Your body is built anew in perfect accord with Mine. Glorify 35
the earth with My presence. *Let the whole body come through.*
Light in all its glory is brought to earth consciously that all
might share My love eternally. The more you allow the Christ
vibration as your life to express *and full-fill Itself,* the more
you become that vibration which is light and unity.

The Christ dimension is building Its own body: a body 36
that is lighter, less dense than the planetary body you are
accustomed to. Show forth My light. Be *conscious* of it.

With your full acceptance of My light in you as I AM, the 37
vibratory rhythm increases and the dense material body will
fall away. You are in the process of harvesting a new body of
light; this body is connected to the power circuits of your
Universe. This body can travel from station to station
throughout the Cosmos. Come into the light and join the
forces of creation to bring forward the embodiment of Creator
in Man.

You are light. You are My Christ, the very essence of 38
My Being in expression right now. When you look to the
Christ within, the GodSelf, I AM in expression for the good
of all. Begin to establish your authority in that body of light.
It is the body I AM giving you as Myself. Take up residence
in Me.

**I AM
With
You**

You are the Creator within. You have powers you have not 39
used and these powers rise up now into your awareness as the
body change takes place. My wisdom governs these powers.
There is no gateway other than through Me. I activate those
powers. I give them back to you as you take up residence
in Me.

It is through My Voice that these powers will be released. 40
You will speak in My name—in My rhythm—and in the sacred
and precise rhythm of your Universe Creator. I, as the GodSelf
you are, command from the center of My Self. I release these
powers into vibration, correcting the misuse of planetary

energy. I use My powers collectively with My Spirit and all things are made whole in Me.

From out of your Self, your divine being, these powers are 41 rising in collective expression, flushing out the old misuse of energy not qualified or applicable any more. The rhythms have changed on your planet Earth. Therefore *new laws come.* Read My new laws to the multitudes.

Take your place in the collective change as gravity is broken 42 and a new gravity circuit is established in a rhythm that is complementary to My Inner Voice, My government in you. I have established a star system that can rejoice with you in the glory of a new day of light and love.

Recall what I have said here. Permit Me to say it again. I 43 gain access through the throat. I release Myself through your throat center, *bringing new powers into fruition.* Place these powers directly in My Hand: the Hand of divine intelligence, the Hand of universal love. Then the prayer that is in your heart becomes the word of God, reissued in My Spirit. It is spoken from the very center of all creation into manifestation to bring hope and joy to all. My creative power is rising to be spoken.

Put On The Immortal Body   You are released of all karma in the Christed way, the way 44 that Jesus taught and demonstrated to you as the Order of Melchizedek. Be conscious of that and unite with others like yourself in the full recognition and movement of the light body.

Be conscious of the body of light as it rapidly assimilates 45 that which you have called "body" and releases you from that "beast" of material vibration. Be the light vibration of My Word. Feast on the light of the Incoming Christ.

I AM Waiting   Do not concern yourself with what you should eat or what 46 you should drink but rather how to feed My young. I call to them but they do not hear Me. With this Bread of Life I give to you, feed them. Let them be clothed and warmed. They will know Me by your touch. They are impoverished by fear and they know not My Hand upon them save by your caring love.

I AM in created form as the rhythm of your existence. I 47 objectify through you as the Kingdom. I AM prepared to receive all people as one in harmony with Myself. I AM prepared to receive all people into My Kingdom *as one flesh.* That is My gift to them. My children will awaken to the glorious Be-coming in the heart. They will have the Creator in them moving and breathing as I AM. I shall show them forth as My people, as rhythm of My existence. As the second coming through all.

I bring up a new form and this form shines with the radiance 48 of who I AM. I announce to you that many suns will arise and they shall be called *My Body of Christ.* They will be as ones who are lighted as cells of My own Being. And My Breath will be upon them. And there shall be no war.

Enter My new dimension of light. I have come to take you 49 to a new place in Me.

CHAPTER SIXTY-THREE

The Order of Melchizedek

*The Order of Melchizedek
is the Central Circuit
through which Christ emanates
as The Son.*

1

T he New Testament Bible (John, Chapter 1) states "In 2
the beginning was the Word...." We are informed at the
beginning of that chapter that God is in the midst of us. If
this be so, then Law has descended from Above and it will
stabilize the land we walk on, this earth. It will create new
circuits of energy and permit new creation as heaven descends
to earth.

The descending and emerging heaven is *the world of light,* 3
that which is bestowed by the Son of God. This frequency is
maintained by the Order of Melchizedek and the Priesthood
of Melchizedek. It is important to note here that in the *Book
Of Hebrews* it is recorded many times that Jesus is High Priest
after the Order of Melchizedek.

The Order   From the Great Sun to the Sun in your heart is the 4
Is The Way   divine Breath breathed. And the Breath is the Light of the
world.

The center of your being is the birthplace *of the original* 5
way, the God Consciousness and the rhythm of the Order of
Melchizedek. You have this sacred rhythm, this pulsation of
oneness, when you resume your place in Me.

The last and the first shall be reunited in the Creator, and 6
the I AM presence that is the GodSelf will be known. The
passage of the one to the other, the Alpha and the Omega,
joins all life *after the Order of Melchizedek* and the dependence
on mortal life is over. *You are the circle of Life.*

In the Breath of God you find yourself as Son and Christ, 7
as the Immortal One. In Me you find the answer to everything
and breathe the new life I have created for you as the Sun,
original creation. You are God rhythm and God life.

See now this Order as your creative energy flowing to you, 8
and rest assured that as you return to Me like the "prodigal
son" we, together, breathe new life as One.

Conscious-ness Reflects The Master
God (I AM) in you is the Law, the Word. To activate the 9
Law, which is the presence of the Universe Creator within
you, is to "keep your eye single" to His powerful Being, His
powerful rhythm and rule. All else fades away but this. For
He has entered this Earth in order to personally reclaim the
Earth and all upon her. And this is to be done now. In fact we
are in the process of this wondrous change.

With Him have arrived many Melchizedek Teacher Sons 10
and Daughters. Righteous Ones who collectively embody the
Creator's Voice and join with Him to foster a new order of
perfection upon this Earth. This is the unseating of the lie.

Where you are, I AM. We are One. In your memory you 11
will know I speak the truth. All the light surrounds My words
and delivers them. They, My words, are moved by My will.
The elected Council of Melchizedek shelters all Melchizedek
light and does not anticipate disaster of any kind. Therefore,
do not give credence to the prophecies of disaster. *There are
none.*

Those who are now carrying My Voice and know My Voice 12
within them are the parts of Me that I call My Council. To
know this Voice is to serve as My Council, to unite all people

in Me as My Son. Hold My hand and we will walk together, you and I, as one being. Giving light to all.

Based on the new circuitry, you have new laws to learn and 13 to understand, universal laws of manifestation and unification. They are not man's law. And in this placement of Law Universal, no thought goes to mortal life, no thought to "self." As you—humanity—move together as a collective body, I set a new rhythm out of Myself that is the Melchizedek Record come to life. It is the Presence of the Master in you as I AM.

The GodSelf Workbook will be available in June 1999.
Workbook questions and exercises assist to reinforce the truth
principles presented in *The GodSelf* and to inspire ongoing
realization and revelation. Other publications by
Patricia Jepsen Chuse include a series of correspondence courses
which are published by the University of Melchizedek.
For further information or to order the courses and workbook,
contact:

Patricia Jepsen Chuse
P.O. Box 36330
Tucson, Arizona 85740

or order online at
www.newlearning.org